Blockchain Oracles and the Oracle Problem

*A practical handbook to discover the world of blockchain, smart contracts, and oracles
—exploring the limits of trust decentralization.*

Written by Giulio Caldarelli

Disclaimer

The information contained in this book is intended only for educational and general information purposes.

None of the information provided is intended as financial or entrepreneurial advice.

The author has no link with any of the companies mentioned in the book. Related reasonings and discussions should not be interpreted as preferential choices. Furthermore, the author takes no responsibility for consequences deriving from the misinterpretation of the provided material. Companies cited in this book, such as Chainlink, Augur, Provable, and Delphi, were informed and received the text before publication.

This book does not encourage any form of investment into blockchains or cryptocurrencies. As early-stage technologies, any related investment has to be considered highly risky.

The narrative of this book may be biased by personal experience with blockchain technologies. Thus, I sincerely encourage you to read related books by other authors and to gather information from different viewpoints.

General Info

The front cover of the book was designed by Giacomo Molè
www.giacomomole.it

The pictures inside the book were created by the author using Microsoft PowerPoint. Vector image licenses were open access or legally acquired.

Open access vector sources: openclipart.org, publicdomainvectors.org

Licensed vector source: vectorstock.com

The text has been checked by the Scribendi professional proofreading service: www.scribendi.com

ISBN 979-12-200-8338-6

Edition, 1.07

Errors

Please contact me if you find any errors.

While every possible effort has been made to ensure the quality and accuracy of the content, spelling, grammar, and other mistakes are often missed in the early version of the manuscript.

I would deeply appreciate it if you could contact me directly if you notice any mistakes before taking any other action. This would allow me to quickly fix these errors before they negatively impact the image of the book.

Accordingly, if you do not share some of the points of view discussed in the book, or if you have other perspectives that you believe are important to add, please send those to me as well. If pertinent and enlightening, they could be added into future editions.

Contact: giuliocaldarelli187@gmail.com

Contact and feedback

Although I have already published academic papers on the subject, this is my first book about blockchain technology. I encourage you to leave feedback if you like the content and to advise if any parts of the book need improvement.

Email   giuliocaldarelli187@gmail.com

I normally do not use social media, but you can find me on **LinkedIn** and **ResearchGate**. Feel free to connect!

Preface

This book seeks to raise awareness about blockchain oracles and the oracle problem. Although I am deeply engaged in writing and publishing academic articles on this thrilling yet controversial topic, I felt compelled to provide accessible resources with a more general audience in mind.

Although most of my academic publications are open-source (and thus freely accessible to anyone), their language and methodology are meant for an academic readership. The content of scholarly articles is typically directed to people already involved in research, presenting the latest results and innovations. With this book, I wanted to 'press pause' on the academic writing and explain or summarize this content in simple, colloquial language. I am aware that there are already many books on blockchains and smart contracts; I wanted my readers (regardless of their background) to gain practical knowledge about oracles, oracle problems, and real-world blockchains. For some reason, although these topics are well known by insiders, they are rarely discussed and addressed in the official channels.

On the one hand, as an academic, I am attempting to contribute to solutions to the oracle problem; on the other hand, I believe this problem is too big for a restricted number of people to work on. It is only with the cooperation of academics, practitioners, and enthusiasts from all research and study fields that we might effectively address the oracle problem and aim for widespread adoption of real-world blockchains.

Although this book mainly considers oracles and oracle problems, I also wanted to provide a stand-alone resource for those who have never heard of blockchains. Thus, the book's opening sections are dedicated to explaining what a blockchain is and how we arrived at smart contracts. This also places the role of oracles in context, and when their presence constitutes a problem. Throughout the book, I refer to examples, comparisons, and conjectures that are generally avoided in academic articles, but which are useful and necessary to understand various aspects of the technology.

A final note about the content of the book: although I am a technology enthusiast, my background is in economics and social sciences, so I will not go into overly technical details. However, I will try to explain how these technologies operate and why they are important from the perspective of a non-engineer. For this reason, I believe that this book is better suited for students and others with a social sciences background. Entrepreneurs and crypto-enthusiasts are also welcome to read the book, and I hope it acts as a source of inspiration. Lastly, while I do not think that the provided knowledge will add any greater understanding to engineers, software developers, and highly skilled people in the blockchain field, if they do decide to spend their time reading the book, I would really appreciate their feedback on its content.

Whoever you are, thank you very much for reading my book!

Table of Contents

Introduction

Blockchain has clearly become a trending topic. The problem is that there is still no official guide or resource that everyone agrees on as the correct or most accessible background material on the subject.

Personally, I think everyone in this domain has had difficulties searching for a starting point or a trusted base from which to learn. Most of the people who now consider themselves well versed probably cannot remember how they started to learn about the topic. In reality, there were no knowledge repositories for the early adopters; they had to learn by doing.

While I consider myself an enthusiast of the technology, I am not an early adopter, so I remember perfectly how and when I came in contact with blockchain and cryptocurrencies. I remember that I was so caught up in my daily life that, even if I heard about Bitcoin, Ethereum, and related topics, I never even gave them a second look.

I first came in contact with the Bitcoin blockchain in the academic year 2016–17. At the time, I was teaching business administration, finance, and marketing in a high school. That year, I gave the usual homework to my finance students: after explaining the theory and fundamentals of finance and financial products, I provided them with an educational platform charged with $20,000 of test money and asked them to invest it. They had to take note of every investment and explain their reasoning. After a given amount of time, they then had to monitor how their investment had performed and write a report explaining the reasons behind the favorable/unfavorable fluctuation of their assets. That particular year, one of the final reports really grabbed my attention. The student in question had "this Bitcoin thing" among his investments. In the report, he explained that he chose to buy this asset because he had read that a group of hackers was threatening companies and asking for ransoms to be paid in Bitcoin.

He argued that if companies were to pay the ransom, they had to buy more Bitcoin, eventually fueling demand for the asset as well as its price.

Since I studied cybersecurity after my own graduation, I was intrigued. I remember going home asking myself: *What is this Bitcoin?*

I am not ashamed to say that, at the time, I was convinced that blockchain was a sort of artificial intelligence meant to automate investment in, and thus guarantee a great profit for Bitcoin. Given all the scams and false advertising online, I believe many people were thinking the same about this world and technology. But from that episode on, I started literally devouring books, articles, and online content about blockchain, so much so that I also decided to enter academia to investigate the subject further.

Blockchain was advertised as a disruptive technology that could completely change the supply chain sector. For example, as an academic, my colleagues and I dealt with blockchain implemented for the traceability of products like food and clothes. By this point, many academic papers had discussed the importance of blockchain to trace the origin of products securely and transparently, so that customers could be certain about what they were buying. I also attended a course on blockchain at the University of Nicosia in Cyprus, where blockchain use for product traceability was one of the many subjects of discussion. It was there that I first heard about *the oracle problem*: since uploading real-world data to the blockchain requires oracles controlled by the companies involved, there could be no guarantee that the data found on the blockchain is true.

Despite all my research up to this point, I had never heard about oracles or the oracle problem. Since it was a brand new and exciting subject, I decided to focus all my efforts on blockchain oracles and the oracle problem. After collecting more data and knowledge on the subject, I also wrote and published a number of papers outlining my research. Luckily, I also had the chance to present and discuss the issue at several international conferences.

With this book, I want to spread this knowledge outside academia and, in particular, to speak to those without a technical background.

The book is organized into six chapters, divided according to the subject of discussion.

Chapter 1 gives an overview of blockchain technology and the Bitcoin cryptocurrency.

Chapter 2 introduces the concept of smart contracts and explains the motives behind the creation of the alternative blockchain named Ethereum, which are both fundamental to understanding the needs of oracles.

Chapters 3 and 4 then turn to the oracles and the oracle problem, respectively. These constitute the core of the book and the starting point for further discussion.

Chapter 5 outlines certain active projects or proposals for managing oracles and addressing the oracle problem. Although it was impossible to avoid mentioning the name of the companies involved, as explained in the disclaimer, the information provided should not be intended as an advertisement, since the discussion does not involve an assessment of the companies. Accordingly, those projects not mentioned are not considered worse; more likely, they will be discussed in future editions.

Finally, Chapter 6 considers several real-world application cases of the oracles and the oracle problem from fields such as intellectual property, academic transcripts, the supply chain, healthcare, and resource management. As I tried some of these applications myself, I will also describe my personal experiences as well as related ongoing challenges.

I hope you enjoy the reading!

Chapter 1

What is a blockchain?

The hype around blockchain arose after the price of Bitcoin became relevant (2014 – 2017), and its user base expanded from restricted groups of geeks to professional investors, banks, institutions, and even governments.

But from an historical point of view, it all started when a man (or group of people) under the pseudonym Satoshi Nakamoto published a whitepaper entitled "Bitcoin: A Peer-to-Peer Electronic Cash System." Satoshi Nakamoto's true identity remains unknown to the public, as his online activity stopped on April 23, 2011, with the message, *"I've moved on to other things. [Bitcoin]'s in good hands with Gavin and everyone."* Discussion among academics on the origin of Nakamoto's *chain of blocks* also points back to the 1990s, citing a project by Haber and Stornetta. Others have even considered the distributed ledger mechanisms used by the Roman Empire.

While the origin of the Bitcoin cryptocurrency can be traced back to 2008, its underlying blockchain technologies are separated by decades or even centuries. Of course, understanding the potential of blockchain cannot be separated from its first famous application: Bitcoin. But Bitcoin was not the first cryptocurrency ever created or developed; there have been similar experiments since the advent of the Internet. However, the central problem of making a digital currency lies in a common property of digital files: replicability.

A digital currency can easily be replicated just like any other digital file, leading to the problem of *double-spending*. The software used to generate currency could also easily be destroyed, altered, or exploited by its developer or other malicious entities. In fact, the main reason the bitcoin cryptocurrency survived and obtained its current value is that it managed to address and prevent (at least until now) all these issues.

This chapter outlines how the Bitcoin blockchain works and how it successfully mitigated the double-spending problem. Although it is about technical things, I promise that it is not too technical!

Underlying technologies

Peer-to-peer: Peer-to-peer technology became famous in the early 2000s thanks to illegal music sharing programs like Napster and WinMX. It permits direct communication between clients (peers) to share data without the intervention of a central server. To give an example, even when we use messaging software like WhatsApp or Facebook Messenger, we are not communicating directly with the other person. Our messages are first sent to the software server and then redirected to our contacts.

In essence, peer-to-peer technologies allow our data (be it messages or files) to be directly transmitted to our interlocutor. Although time-saving is one obvious advantage, there are other benefits, specifically regarding how the presence of a third party may affect the data transmitted. First, the third party can observe all the shared data, which de facto violates user privacy. Second, a central server may prevent certain users from accessing the service due to blacklisting. Third, there is no guarantee that these middlemen have not altered the data. In response, peer-to-peer technology ensures that shared data is direct, non-modified, and (to a certain extent) private.

Cryptography: The word *cryptography* comes from Greek and literally means 'hidden writing' (*Kryptos/Graphein*). Both the need to hide writing and the art of doing so have ancient origins. The most ancient known use of cryptography was found in an inscription carved, in around 1900 BC, in the main hall of the tomb of the Egyptian Great Chief Khnumhotep II. The inscription used some unusual form of hieroglyphics in place of the ordinary ones.

The most famous example of cryptography, however, dates back to 100 BC. Julius Caesar was known to use a form of encryption to send secret messages to his army generals. His cryptographic technique took the name of the *Caesar cipher*. This elementary form of cipher requires that the letters forming a message are substituted for other characters according to a common rule. For example, if our cryptographic rule is $a + 2$, we would substitute the letters from our message with those following in the alphabet plus one.

a
THE KEY IS IN THE RED CABINET

a+1
UIF LFZ JT JO UIF SFE DBCJOFU

a+2
VJG MGA KU KP VJG TGF ECDKPGV

As a result, a message like "the key is in the red cabinet" would be displayed as "vjg mga ku kp vjg tgf ecdkpgv." If the receiver knows the decrypting key is $a + 2$, the information can easily be decrypted. However, as time passed, encryption techniques became more and more sophisticated. With the introduction of machines, rules, and patterns became increasingly difficult for humans to decode. During World War II, Alan Turing's breaking of the Nazi Enigma code at Bletchley Park is a prime example of cryptography's evolution and its implications.[1]

---

[1] I strongly encourage you to watch the 2014 film *The Imitation Game*, which dramatizes this very subject.

Reasons for hiding a message can be infinite. Ultimately, cryptography helps provide accountability, fairness, accuracy, and confidentiality. It is especially useful in preventing fraud in electronic commerce and concealing information from those not involved in the communication or transaction.

Distributed ledger technologies: The simplest way to understand distributed ledger technologies is to start with its closest corollary: cloud computing. Not that long ago, if we had a document that we could not afford to lose or we needed to access anywhere, the easiest and safest option was to send them to our own email address. That way, if we accessed our inbox from any PC, laptop, or smartphone, we could also have access to our important documents. The premise here was to exploit the storage offered by our email provider to store documents; we were essentially reliant on a third party to keep our files accessible. This idea was then exploited by the Dropbox startup, which launched its now ubiquitous software in 2008.

Since Dropbox, all the tech giants have offered cloud computing services for storing our data. Think Google's Drive or Microsoft's OneDrive. With cloud computing, our data is stored on a secure server, accessible from anywhere in the world—even if we lose our device or travel without our physical hard drives. Nowadays, cloud computing technology is also capable of executing programs in the cloud, so it offers more than the mere storage of data.

On the flipside, the limitation of cloud computing is that our data is still centralized on the server, even if stored by a third party. Although it seems unlikely, there is still a chance of losing our data if the server fails or is attacked. Distributed ledger technologies offer all the cloud computing innovations with the added advantage that data is stored across multiple devices belonging to different entities[2]. This means that our data is safe

---

[2] Cloud computing may also use multiple or virtual servers. However they are all controlled by the same entity.

and accessible by all our devices anywhere, even if one or multiple servers are shut down.

Consensus Mechanism: In any central storage or database, a central authority has the right to decide whether data can be added, deleted, or updated. When a database is distributed, there is no such authority, so there is a need to obtain an agreement as to which pieces of data should be added and which should be excluded.

The Byzantine Generals problem is often used to illustrate the difficulty of reaching a decentralized consensus. In this problem, our generals are ready to attack a city from four directions. However, they are unable to communicate with each other and coordinate their movements. They know that if they all attack simultaneously, they will succeed; if some do not attack or delay their assault, they will fail. The only way for the generals to communicate with each other is by an emissary, but once the emissary arrives with the information, they will never know whether the information is correct or if the emissary is really a spy from the city. This quandary is comparable to reaching a consensus in the context of a public database, where people do not know or trust each other. In response, a consensus mechanism is a set of predetermined rules accepted by all participants to reach the necessary agreement.

Chain of blocks: Named as such by Nakamoto, this is an ideal graphical representation of the ledger that constitutes the so-called blockchain. Data is stored in *blocks*, and those that connect to each other form a *chain*. Although it is always represented this way in books, advertising, and online, the chain is really only a suggestion to better understand how the database works and how it is structured. In reality, no database takes the tangible form of a chain, nor is it represented this way by a software explorer. Looking at a computer or server from the outside, we cannot determine if it is running a blockchain or a legacy database.

The above-mentioned technologies are only the most discussed in blockchain. Of course, none of this would have been possible without the

Internet and its unparalleled level of development and distribution. Although it would be possible to operate on the Bitcoin blockchain using phone SMS, the whole system could not be launched in a world with a slow and scattered Internet connection.

The Bitcoin blockchain

The Bitcoin blockchain is undoubtedly the most widely recognized. In many books, it is used as a general example to explain how blockchain works. However, the Bitcoin blockchain has its own peculiar characteristics.

More specifically, the Bitcoin blockchain is:

Open—The Bitcoin blockchain is accessible to anyone, for free. Virtually, it is also accessible by any device regardless of technological advancement. Although it is easier to access a Bitcoin wallet with an advanced device with a fast Internet connection, it is also possible to create Bitcoin transactions without an Internet connection using an older cellphone and SMS technology.

Borderless—It does not matter if the transactions on the Bitcoin blockchain occur in the same room or between the two poles; the distance between users does not affect the functioning of the platform in any way. This is definitely an advantage for people transacting across significant distances. Conversely, of course, it is a limitation for people transacting face to face, who do not experience a faster transaction.

Immutable—Unlike common databases, the Bitcoin blockchain is specifically designed to be unalterable. This means that, even if it is possible to write and add new data, it is impossible to erase blocks. As a result, the transaction history cannot be deleted.

Transparent—The Bitcoin blockchain is freely auditable by anyone. Regular use is not a requirement, either: all that is needed is an Internet connection and some basic knowledge. In this way, anyone can access the Bitcoin blockchain ledger and verify the truthfulness of transactions.

Censorship resistance—The absence of a central authority in the Bitcoin blockchain makes it impossible for certain users or transactions to be denied or prevented. The only thing that matters is that the escrow shows a positive balance, and fees are paid. The reasons why the cryptocurrency is transferred or the nature of the people involved do not matter at all. Likewise, the purpose of a transaction does not affect its outcome. Anyone (or anything) can gain access to the blockchain, whether human, or AI.

Pseudonymous—Participation in the blockchain is not anonymous. Rather, it is based on a pseudonym. For example, if our pseudonym is 1337, as long as nobody knows that it belongs to us, we will benefit from anonymous transactions. But from the moment the alias becomes associated with us, our transactions will no longer be anonymous.

Again, it is imperative to specify that these characteristics belong only to the Bitcoin blockchain. And while many books, articles, and tutorials associate these characteristics with regular blockchain technologies, in reality, these can be of infinite types and characteristics. In other words, many misconceptions about the technology arise because of the overlap between generic blockchain characteristics and those of Bitcoin specifically. In fact, blockchain has no intrinsic characteristics per se; it all depends on how it is developed.

How the Bitcoin blockchain works

Nodes and the genesis block

The Bitcoin blockchain, then, is a system made to support a specific cryptocurrency. While someone knows that it is possible to freely download the blockchain and execute and verify all transactions, others may know that a new block is added every ten minutes and that, sometimes, new blocks are added simultaneously. The following section aims to bring everything together and hopefully give a complete overview of how the Bitcoin blockchain operates.

Nakamoto's Bitcoin whitepaper was first published in 2008. However, blockchain deployment truly began with the creation of the first block, known as the *genesis block*. Nakamoto himself was most likely its architect.

Along with the data, the genesis block contained the following sentence: *"The Times 03/Jan/2009 Chancellor on brink of second bailout for banks."* The motives behind this choice are still unknown, but the news and date were probably chosen to pinpoint the blockchain's exact deployment.

While anyone can freely access and download the software and the entire blockchain, those who run it are called *nodes*. Crucially, a node passively contributes to the system but does not receive any sort of compensation. The only entity who does receive compensation whenever a new block is added is the *miner*.

Blocks, miners, and proof-of-work

Each block has limited storage of 1 megabyte and is meant to contain transactional data. When created, it bears an exact timestamp (in the format YYYY-MM-DD hh:mm), which facilitates its position within the chain. In the case of Bitcoin, since the scope of the blockchain was to provide a peer-to-peer electronic cash system, the platform is specifically intended to contain data about Bitcoin transactions.

Below is an example of data within a block:[3]

---

[3] Taken from https://www.blockchain.com/explorer.

Block 665563 ⓘ

Hash	0000000000000000000c25d6d9a18a2782d711adbba7f0556614d15dd19680d3 📋
Confirmations	2
Timestamp	2021-01-11 11:11
Height	665563
Miner	Unknown
Number of Transactions	2,368
Difficulty	20,607,418,304,385.63
Merkle root	31b9686d9c6b49a4a206db7b8df76061e9c4822e418f81ad61a900a0b9d9e443
Version	0x20000000
Bits	386,771,105
Weight	3,993,531 WU
Size	1,130,433 bytes
Nonce	3,581,014,400
Transaction Volume	1180.64329664 BTC
Block Reward	6.25000000 BTC
Fee Reward	0.31240436 BTC

Block Transactions ⓘ

Hash	5ab997a4776f9e346fd58868f703a1bfd4c57cc113407e2bd482b9e…			2021-01-11 11:11
	COINBASE (Newly Generated Coins)	⇒	bc1qjl8uwezzlech723ipnyuza0h2cdkvxvh54v3… Unable to decode output address Unable to decode output address Unable to decode output address	6.56240436 BTC
Fee	0.00000000 BTC (0.000 sat/B - 0.000 sat/WU - 340 bytes)			6.56240436 BTC
				2 Confirmations

Hash	a554ec725bfda8933145c0a0c33212303a5aaa35e34442b7aa8fb1…			2021-01-11 11:02
	bc1qfnt48f4ytcesqagkgl4qs0ewudr6khrpgn39… 19.25118307 BTC	⇒	123rdDmH5FY2NgBCyCFFCbq9UJeWmBDrr8 1FhfZwejmEnTB41c63oDrdkJ84ChuHHRSK 3PQubkKYq8YpQWxfpp8MK5jPufvFMrfPbs bc1qwspucrmmdsaufsh3d839ay0lnejk259pl9…	0.00468696 BTC 0.01016737 BTC 0.02300000 BTC 19.21227874 BTC
Fee	0.00105000 BTC (359.589 sat/B - 125.298 sat/WU - 292 bytes)			19.25013307 BTC
				2 Confirmations

Hash	8ff5d4e8e4fc7d8fbfe2fbd3b55dcceb200204e89e941ac718e9582c…			2021-01-11 11:02
	17A16QmavnUfCW11DAApiJxp7ARnxN5pGX 29.88381817 BTC	⇒	36U4CnzwxLaL9pUcobsXoastruQQpc3UZs 3HsUi9uzq2bBonxAkXH22uV4SbK9KD3eQy 17A16QmavnUfCW11DAApiJxp7ARnxN5pGX	0.00025377 BTC 0.00826664 BTC 29.87423577 BTC
Fee	0.00106199 BTC (370.031 sat/B - 92.508 sat/WU - 287 bytes)			29.88275618 BTC
				2 Confirmations

After a certain number of transactions, a new block needs to be generated and added to the chain. Because the blockchain is public and without central authority, anyone can provide a new block to be added to the chain, with different transactions and fees. To decide which block should be added, Nakamoto outlines the consensus mechanism required to proceed to the final agreement. For the Bitcoin blockchain, the chosen consensus mechanism is *proof-of-work*.

The proof-of-work is an old technology used during the email era to prevent spam, in which the server required the client to execute a small puzzle to be able to send the email. Since the solution to the puzzle required a certain amount of computing power, it would have been very wasteful to send many emails in a row. The principle here is to increase the effort required to complete a single action, thereby preventing a system overload.

With Bitcoin, the addition of a new block also requires solving a puzzle. The nodes who actively work to solve this puzzle and add the resulting blocks are called *miners*. Since only one block is added (and rewarded) at a time, miners must compete with each other. All the miners want to add the new block, as the one who wins receives the fees of the transactions as well as newly minted Bitcoin.[4]

Since solving the puzzle consumes computing power, as the price of Bitcoin has increased, more and more people have joined the group of miners. Ad hoc processors called ASIC[5] were also built to mine Bitcoin and to have more chances to add blocks.

However, the Bitcoin software is made specifically to allow the addition of a new block only every ten minutes. For this reason, the difficulty of the puzzle is adjusted and increased if the total computing power of the miners results in a *block time* under 10 minutes.

On the other hand, if the miners' total computing power decreases and the block time increases, the puzzle's difficulty is automatically reduced. Since miners do not work in coordination, two different miners may add a block at the same time. Other miners then have to choose where to add a new block. When the new block is mined, the other branch is left behind (as orphaned blocks)[6]. Subsequent blocks will always be added to the longest chain:

---

[4] Minting is the technical term for the issuance of cryptocurrencies. Mining, on the other hand, refers to the specific activity of miners who perform the proof-of-work to validate a block. The transaction that generates a newly minted Bitcoin is called the *coinbase transaction*.

[5] Application Specific Integrated Circuit.

[6] Miners of the orphaned blocks are not rewarded so it is essential to chose the right branch

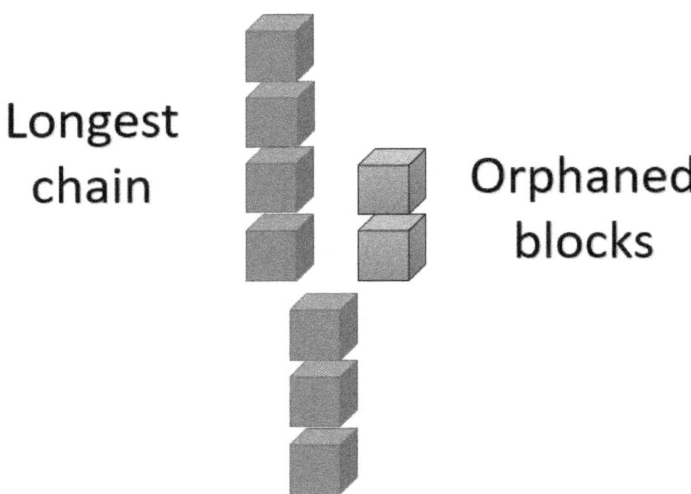

There is also the case in which miners deliberately split the chain into two because they have different views of the blockchain rules. Here, the miners will continue to mine both branches of the chain. The blockchain is then *forked*, and although the two branches share the same history, they will follow different futures. A famous example of this premise is the Bitcoin Cash blockchain (BCH):

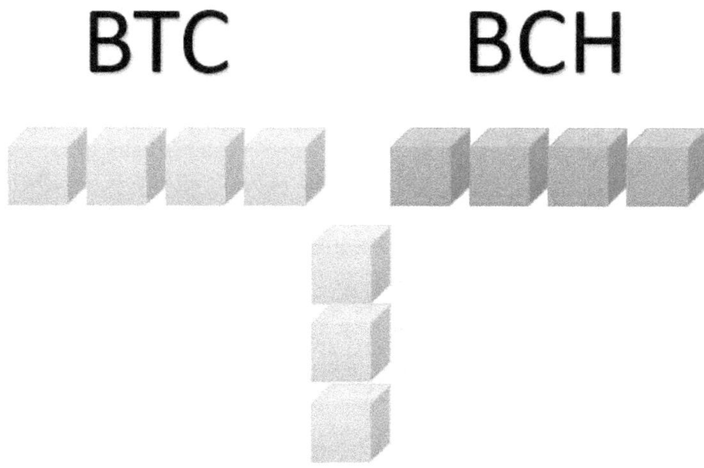

Personally, I have read many books about the functioning of the Bitcoin blockchain and proof-of-work, but honestly, the mechanism only became clear after a professor showed me an internet simulator that I would happily share with you. In the appendix of this book, I outline the simulator's procedure, but I would also invite you to visit the website and try it out for yourself. I can guarantee that running the simulator is way more straightforward than reading hundreds of sources.

Furthermore, I have decided not to explain the concepts of hash and cryptography within the Bitcoin blockchain any further here, since both will be more comprehensible when using the simulator.

Wallets, address, transactions, and fees

Those who run a full node can also create a Bitcoin wallet. For every wallet created, the system will release a pair of two keys: one private and one public.

Below is an example of public and private keys generated at bitaddress.org:

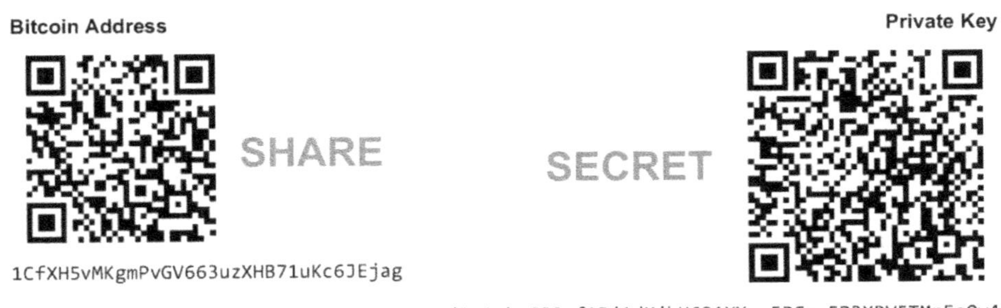

These are real sets of keys[7]. As clearly indicated, one (Bitcoin Address) can and should be shared. The other (Private Key) must be kept secret and not shared with anyone. The public key is used to generate the address that can be shared during a payment or an auditing procedure. Significantly,

---

[7] Since these keys are shared publicly in this book, please do not use them as anyone would have access to your funds!

anyone can use an address to audit the corresponding transactions. Auditing blockchain transactions is simple and can be done by anyone, whether they are Bitcoin stakeholders or not. The simplest way to inspect the blockchain is to use an explorer, such as the one found at blockchain.com/explorer.

As the above-generated address will have no transactions, below I will inspect a random address found online:

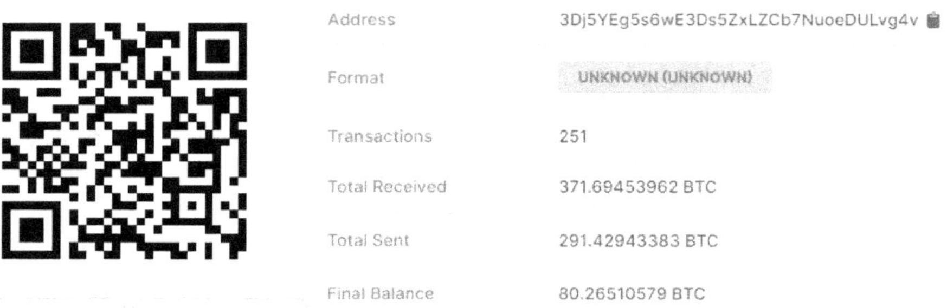

This image displays an address that shows 251 transactions since its generation, along with total amounts of Bitcoin received (371) and spent (291). It also gives information on the actual balance, which is a little over 80 Bitcoin.

The figure below displays all the transactions involving this address, whether they are incoming or outgoing.

Hash	8008f30149f0bce4879cb5b89e2b113ec65...		2020-12-22 12:06
	3Q2nVw7odxLKEok7qB... 0.00452802 BTC	37zR3peNYauC6AwjzjY... 0.00570240 BTC	
	3Dj5YEg5s6wE3Ds5Zx... 0.00457658 BTC	3Dj5YEg5s6wE3Ds5Zx... 0.00751548 BTC	
	3Dj5YEg5s6wE3Ds5Zx... 0.00501088 BTC		
Fee	0.00089760 BTC (152.136 sat/B - 64.669 sat/WU - 590 bytes)		-0.00207198 BTC

Hash	ce4af0bd97179477ec9167dc2ed253ea510d...		2020-12-22 12:08
	3NeeowPFvuhfEZPPCL... 0.00518879 BTC	33Vbuh7FKe7sNhu22q... 0.00847072 BTC	
	396vQBnUq5qxgyoGLg... 0.00520000 BTC	3Dj5YEg5s6wE3Ds5Zx... 0.00706047 BTC	
	32e215ac9G1TtRdLyh2... 0.00604000 BTC		
Fee	0.00089760 BTC (152.136 sat/B - 64.669 sat/WU - 590 bytes)		+0.00706047 BTC

← 2 3 **4** 5 6 +10 →

As well as the transactions listed, by browsing the pages, we have access to all of them. In the lower-left corner, we can also see the fees paid to the miner; on the lower right, we can see the outcome of the transaction (positive or negative).

So, to receive Bitcoin, it is both necessary and sufficient to share our address or *public key*. Anyone who knows our public key can send us a payment, even against our will. In fact, receiving a payment requires no special operation on our part. Indeed, when the price of Bitcoin was very low, it was pretty common to see people posting their public key on social media, asking for cryptocurrency payments. And according to what they say, they actually received them!

To send a payment, we need to have access to our *private key*. Anyone in possession of the private key of an address has the right to operate it. This is a fundamental concept in Bitcoin. Access to the private key is all that matters. If you lose access to the private key, for whatever reason, you will lose access to your Bitcoin, forever. There is no password reset button for the Bitcoin blockchain.

When sending a payment, it is sufficient to insert the receiver address (public key) or scan its QR code, then select the amount of Bitcoin to send. Finally, we must 'choose' the fees.

The concept of fees should not be new to us. Whenever we want to perform an operation in society, for example, an international transfer of funds, someone will tell us the rules. We must fill out some forms used for identification (like Know Your Customer, or KYC) and for anti-money laundering (AML), until eventually we are informed of the predetermined fees required to complete the transaction.

In Bitcoin, however, since there is no central authority, no one decides the amount of fees incurred. Instead, the amount of fees that we choose to add to our transaction will only determine the speed at which the transaction will be added to the blockchain and confirmed. Since each block is limited to 1 megabyte, the miners will prioritize the transactions with the highest amount of fees and postpone those with the lowest. Sending a payment with very low transaction fees will also delay the confirmation; if the miners do not process it in time, it may also be rejected (typically after 14 days). On the other hand, adding a decent amount of fees to our transaction will cause it to be processed first. There is no limit to the fees that may be added to a transaction, so it is important to double-check the amount. It is common, for example, for the number of fees to be inverted with the payment. Unfortunately, when this happens, the transaction is often prioritized, making it impossible to make changes.

To open a wallet, it is not necessary to manage a full node, as there are many other simpler alternatives. Paper, web, and phone wallets are the most common, but the most recommended type remains *cold storage*. Storage is defined as "cold" when it has no access to the Internet, making it highly unlikely to be hacked. The last but also the most important thing to know about a wallet is that no identification is required. Anyone, human, or AI can use Bitcoin, and the system will never require any identification document to operate it.

Block time, halving, and the Bitcoin cap

The total amount of Bitcoin ever issuable is limited to 21 million[8] and predetermined by the software. The reasons for this choice are unknown, but the capped amount is probably meant to give a deflationary nature to Bitcoin, in contrast to our usual currencies (e.g., $, ¥, €, £).

As explained earlier, whenever a block is added to the chain by a miner, new Bitcoin are issued by the system. The number of issued Bitcoin, however, varies with time. When the platform was launched, the block reward was 50 Bitcoin, but this has now decreased after various rounds of *halving*, a process in which the block reward is halved, and which demands further explanation.

I remember that, before the last halving, I was watching a YouTube video that explained how the process worked. The YouTuber said that halving happens every three years and bore the brunt of many negative comments from people saying it was every four years. Technically speaking, neither position is right nor wrong. This is because Bitcoin halving happens exactly after 210,000 blocks have been added, so it has nothing to do with chronological time. However, since the mean block time is ten minutes, the halving can be expected to happen once every four years.

On the other hand, block time is influenced by total computing power. Therefore, although highly improbable, it is not impossible to witness a halving every three or five years. In any case, the block reward will be lower and lower until the complete issue of all Bitcoin, which should happen in around the year 2140 (after the 32nd halving). Many are curious as to what will happen after 2140, and whether the miners will continue to contribute to the system once no new Bitcoin are issued and transaction fees alone make up the block reward.

---

[8] The exact number is 20,999,999.9769. Source: Andreas M. Antonopoulos, *Mastering Bitcoin: Unlocking Digital Crypto-Currencies* (Cambridge, MA: O'Reilly Media, 2014).

Today (in 2021), the issued Bitcoin are usually worth more than the transaction fees, but this will inevitably shift. Indeed, it is likely that, after the eighth halving in around 2036, the system will survive with transaction fees alone. The developer's hope is that, by that time, the price of Bitcoin will be so high that the transaction fees alone will be greater than the mining costs.

How and why do Bitcoins have a price?

To better answer these questions, we first need to distinguish the concepts of value and price.

When we go to the supermarket and browse the list of products, we can easily spot a number on the shelf or on the product itself. This is the **price** of the product. The price is the amount of money required to exchange a specific product. If we spot a product that we like at $10 and we have $10 in our purse, we can buy the product by handing our $10 to the cashier.

The concept of value is completely different. Its meaning is not as trivial as its price. The value of a product can be either higher, lower, or equal to its price. Its value will also change according to the time, condition, and person asked to evaluate the product.

To understand the concept of value, let's focus on a resource known to everyone: water. Typically, the value of water is approximately zero, since it is an abundant resource in nature, and it falls from the sky, for free! Supermarkets, on the other hand, sell mineral water at a price that is above zero; for this reason, not everyone is available to pay for it.

Let's imagine that a pack of six bottles of water costs $3 at the supermarket, and our perceived value is $0. We can say that the value is lower than the price, so we are more likely to drink water straight from the tap. But if we have young children and care about how safe the water is, then our perceived value of safe water will more closely match the supermarket price. In this case, we will probably buy just the amount of bottled water we need, because we know there is always a supermarket that can provide more water at the same (or similar) price if we need more.

Let's hypothesize further that water arrives at home only in small quantities due to an aqueduct failure, and its drinkability is not guaranteed. Since water is necessary for our survival but is no longer available for free, its perceived value will start (moderately) to exceed $3. Although the price is likely to still be $3, the perceived value increases proportionally as the supermarket's water supply decreases. As a family, we may also consider buying extra water, fearing a future scarcity.

In an extreme case, if water becomes so scarce that we do not have enough to drink, its perceived value would be far greater than gold (for example), which has no use to dehydrated people. Any remaining water will likely be sold on the black market at a greatly elevated price. By this point, the price at which the water will be sold will depend solely on the maximum price that people are able to spend to procure it.

Now let's try to contextualize these concepts of price and value in the world of Bitcoin. Since they are infinitely replicable, digital entities have no tangible price or value. A digital file cannot have a positive value (> 0), irrespective of how difficult it was to create. As anyone can make a copy, it can be given away for free. Bitcoin's perceived value, however, is potentially positive (> 0) because it is the first digital resource whose availability is not infinite. If we try to replicate a transaction or spend our Bitcoin a second time, the system will perceive the transaction as invalid.

If this explains why Bitcoin has a potentially positive value, it does not explain its price. While it is true that an infinite resource has a value equal to zero, it is not always true that a limited resource has a value above zero. For Bitcoin to obtain value, people must first be interested in it and willing to exchange it for other currencies.

Bitcoin was initially only exchanged on forums of insiders, and it took time for its price to become financially relevant. Its price reached $1 in July 2010 and kept a low profile until 2017, when it reached a considerable price of around \$19,000. The price of Bitcoin also reached another all-time high in 2021 due to the effects of the covid-19 crisis, passing \$60,000. Many experts believe the cost will eventually reach \$100,000, but this will depend on future and unpredictable events. If something breaks the code, the price may also drop to zero in a matter of hours.

One important event in Bitcoin's history finally gave a tangible weight to its value. The event is commonly known as "Pizza Day." On May 22, 2010 (at 21:16:31), a young programmer named Laszlo Hanyecz bought two Papa John's pizzas for 10,000 BTC. Rumor has it that, in particular, the programmer agreed with a third party on bitcointalk[9] to buy the two pizzas on his behalf in exchange for 10,000 BTC (the equivalent of around \$41 at the time). This event is significant because Bitcoin was finally given not only a price but also a commercial market value.

By the time of Pizza Day, the price of Bitcoin had already changed a lot, and it has continued to change rapidly. By 2015, those 10,000 Bitcoin had a value of \$2.4 million; by 2019, they were worth over \$80 million. Those are some expensive pizzas!

Someone may also argue that the price of Bitcoin is determined by the electricity consumed in the mining process. In reality, this is not the case. If the price of Bitcoin falls, then the computing power is also reduced to adequate the expenses for electricity to the price of the currency. On the other hand, if the electricity price increases, bitcoin production will not be altered due to the fixed block time. Therefore this should not make the currency more precious.

Ultimately, then, although it is influenced and supported by a multitude of factors, the price is Bitcoin is determined solely by demand.

---

[9] This is an online forum used by early adopters to share information and thoughts on the nascent cryptocurrency.

It is also important to note that the price of Bitcoin is highly volatile and varies according to the exchange platform and currency.

Exchanges	Bitcoin Price (€) at 11/01/2021 17:50 CET
Bitpanda	25,772.62
Kraken	25,869.59
Change	25,928.90
Binance	26,091.40
Coinbase	24,702.79
Altalix	24,791.80
Etoro	25,991.69
Bitfinex	26,321.42
Bitstamp	26,040.45
Bit2me	26,008.71

The table above shows that, at an exact moment in time (January 11, 2021, at 5:50pm CET),[10] one unit of the Bitcoin cryptocurrency could be exchanged for various prices in Euros depending on the exchange selected. Equally, even on the same exchange, the price of Bitcoin will depend on the exchange currency (e.g., €,$,£,¥) itself. Although highly risky, it is possible for professionals to exploit these divergences to make a profit. This phenomenon is known as *arbitrage*. Financial advice and trading explanations, however, are beyond the scope of this book. (I will probably cover these aspects more extensively in future publications.)

---

[10] Data taken from cryptoradar.co.

Security and sustainability of the Bitcoin blockchain

The Bitcoin blockchain is known to be secure and immutable, but how can that be?

Well, the truth is that the Bitcoin blockchain is not impervious, but the likelihood of a breach or unwanted mutation is very low. The reason can be found in the proof-of-work mechanism.

Let's try to understand what it would take to attack and modify the Bitcoin blockchain. To do so would require a sizable amount of computing power to alter the blocks before other competing miners can add a new one.

If our intention was to revert a transaction that happened 20 blocks before the last one, we should at least be able to re-mine all the 20 blocks plus the newest before someone else is able to mine the next one. Since this is extremely unlikely to happen, if five blocks are added on top of the confirmation of our transaction, the chain can already be considered immutable.

The cost of an attack is another reason why a mutation to the bitcoin blockchain is improbable. On the Internet, hacker attacks are pretty common and widespread. Most of the time, all a hacker needs to make an effective attack is a solid strategy and a bit of patience. But when it comes to Bitcoin, these features, while necessary, will prove insufficient. First, time is against the attacker, since a new block is mined every ten minutes, which increases the difficulty of the attack dramatically. Second, the computing power required to mine blocks is expensive, and if an attack on the blockchain fails (which is highly likely), the cost of the computing power cannot be recovered. As a result, Bitcoin remains the most secure blockchain to date.

In turn, the cost of computing power brings up the consideration of the sustainability of the entire Bitcoin system.

The problem of electricity consumption and the Bitcoin blockchain's subsequent impact on the ecosystem is widely debated in the forums. In principle, the software is not programmed to consume a predetermined amount of energy. As we know, energy consumption depends on the competition between miners: the more miners compete to add the block, the more computing power is required. Recent consumption of electricity by miners has exceeded 75 TWh per year[11], which gives us an idea of the magnitude involved—this is the equivalent to the annual electricity consumption of the population of Chile!

The Bitcoin blockchain has often been criticized for its perceived negative impact on the environment. The truth is that any ecological impact is generated by the mechanism used in our society to produce electricity. Arguably, while the Bitcoin blockchain currently consumes a sky-high level of electricity, the pollution comes from the power plants that produce the energy in the first place. If our energy production were 100% renewable, the environmental impact of Bitcoin would be almost nonexistent.

I use the word 'almost' here because another aspect to consider is the heat energy generated by the miners.

Whenever an electrical appliance is turned on, it heats up. Our PCs, for example, have built-in fan or cooling systems to avoid system failures due to overheating. (In winter, I bet that most of us enjoy the heat coming from a desktop PC, which makes the workstation warmer and more comfortable). Now consider that today's processors used for mining are as big as buildings. Imagine how much heat they must produce and how it impacts the surrounding ecosystem. Again, the Bitcoin software is not directly responsible for the heat produced; it is an effect of how the processors are built. With efficient cooling systems and fewer heating processors, the ecological impact would be negligible.

In the end, we must admit that—even though the Bitcoin software itself is not to blame—in its current form, it has an impact on the environment. For

---

[11] Source: https://digiconomist.net/bitcoin-energy-consumption/.

that reason, experts like Andreas Antonopoulos have ventured that no more than one proof-of-work blockchain can be sustainable in the long run.

Challenges of the Bitcoin ecosystem

As outlined above, the known challenges of the Bitcoin blockchain revolve around its economic and environmental sustainability. But there are other important challenges that cannot be overlooked.

1) **Volatility of price and storage of value:** The price of Bitcoin and other cryptocurrencies is extremely volatile. This means that the price at which we buy a unit or a fraction of a specific coin is subject to sudden and rapid changes. It is therefore difficult to think about cryptocurrencies in terms of trading goods or storing value. If, for example, we set the price of a book at a certain amount of Bitcoin, its price (expressed in other currencies) will be extremely volatile, making it difficult for customers to buy. Today, people who accept Bitcoin use services that automatically adjust the price according to the changing rates, but these services are still not completely efficient. Secondly, if we decide to store value in Bitcoin (instead of gold, for example), there is a chance that its entire value could be lost forever due to a system failure. (It is also possible for it to multiply in value, but no guarantees are given over this.) As such, Bitcoin is typically seen as a high-risk investment rather than a store of value.

2) **Growth rate of the blockchain:** New blocks are added to the blockchain at a rate of one every 10 minutes, and each block has an average capacity of 1 MB. Nothing can be deleted. This means that the blockchain extension is permanently increasing at a rate of approximately 1 MB per 10 min. Compared to 2011, when it was possible to have full blockchain nodes running on a smartphone, it is now already difficult to run a full node on a desktop PC. On the one hand, some experts have argued that Bitcoin's growth rate is

lower than that of storage technology. When the blockchain's size reaches 1 TB, for example, our storage should be able to handle it easily. On the other hand, the problem is more serious for blockchains like Ethereum, whose growth rate exceeds that of storage technology improvements. In less than ten years, the Ethereum blockchain will probably be so large that it will be impossible to manage for non-specialized services. This will surely create a problem of centralization.

3) **Security:** Bitcoin security is very high, but this is a double-edged sword. Since Bitcoin recognizes no ruler and no owner, there is no reset button if a transaction is sent to the wrong address and no mechanism to recover lost private keys. Furthermore, there is no way to prevent malevolent people from utilizing our private keys and using Bitcoin for illegal or inappropriate purposes. These features have always raised concerns for KYC and AML policymakers.

4) **Privacy:** Certainly, Bitcoin has a reputation as a system to make anonymous payments, gangster style. In reality, the system is not wholly anonymous, only *pseudonymous*. As soon as one of our transactions is associated with our identity, the entire stream of all our previous transactions can also be matched to us. So, while the blockchain is transparent and immutable, meaning none of our transactions can be canceled, it only takes one mistake for our privacy to be compromised.

5) **Inheritance:** This is the challenge I found particularly exciting while studying cryptocurrencies, and it is one that is rarely addressed in books and tutorials. I also believe it is one of the major points of failure of the Bitcoin premise and of cryptocurrency systems in general.

6) **Underlying assumption:** The whole Bitcoin ecosystem lives on the assumption that transaction fees will be sufficient to reward the miners in the long run. If that condition is not verified, miners will

inevitably leave the mining process, eventually pushing the system to collapse.

Clearly, blockchain security is dependent on the safe storage of the private key. If a private key is lost, the wallet and the currencies it controls are forfeited forever. Therefore, when a cryptocurrency user dies, the currencies he controls also 'die' with him, since no one will be able to access or use his wallet, assuming he safely stored his private key. As time passes and the early adopters of Bitcoin start to die out, the cryptocurrency will die with them.

There are already certain systems that are based on multiple private keys (M of N multi-signature transactions)[12] or custodial services that help users address this issue. Custodial services work as notaries, but they fail in two ways. First, they only work when someone voluntarily creates a will, so it cannot be applied in the case of accidental or sudden death. Second, it implies the intervention of a third party, who would then take custody of the private key, creating a further problem of wallet privacy and security.

Someone may also argue that private keys can be stored in a sealed envelope and given to the beneficiary through a notary service. While this solution may work, it is unfortunately not realistic. When users acquire digital assets, it's unlikely that they leave them in a wallet.

Average crypto users regularly create new wallets, thus new private keys, continually moving their funds around for investment purposes. It means that in order to retrieve working private keys after a user has passed, the user must regularly update the keys in the envelope and the notary service. Although possible, it is extremely unlikely.

---

[12] Multi-signature wallets require a certain number of keys for a transaction to be sent. For example, if a total of three keys are set, a transaction may require that at least two of them are provided.

Closing remarks

In this chapter, we reviewed the main characteristics of a blockchain and the potential (and potential drawbacks) of cryptocurrency. Payments are the exact purpose of the Bitcoin blockchain. For other purposes, other systems are more suitable. In the next chapter, we turn our attention to smart contracts and the Ethereum ecosystem.

Chapter 2

From blockchain to smart contracts

Bitcoin was only the first known application of blockchain technology, and its potential is likely to transcend the simple transaction of currency.

Agreements performed within the blockchain can be automatic, transparent, immutable, and executed without third-party intervention. Such deals are known as *smart contracts*.

The idea of smart contracts can be traced to a cryptographer named Nick Szabo. Originally conceived in the 1990s, Szabo could not see his vision realized until the blockchain era. The original definition of smart contracts refers to *"a set of promises, specified in digital form, including protocols within which the parties perform on these promises."* Once blockchain arrived, it was recognized as the platform with the highest potential for performing smart contracts, specifically in terms of *"self-executing code [...] that automatically implements the terms of an agreement between parties."*[13]

Although the above definitions are both important and interesting, they do not give a clear indication of what a smart contract is or does. The smart contract is actually a computer program. The word "contract" has no connection with any legal meaning in this context; the presumption that these applications could somehow automate or replace legal agreements has led to widespread confusion on forums. A more appropriate name may have been "smart codes" or "smart software," but smart contracts are what they were called from the beginning, and *"the term somehow stuck."*[14]

---

[13] Vida J. Morkunas, Jeannette Paschen, and Edward Boon, "How Blockchain Technologies Impact Your Business Model," *Business Horizons* 62, no. 3 (2019): 295–306.

[14] Andreas M. Antonopoulos & Gavin Wood, *Mastering Ethereum: Implementing Digital Contracts* (Cambridge, MA: O'Reilly, 2018), 127.

Indeed, the adjective "smart" is not especially pertinent either, as it suggests some form of AI that these codes do not have.

The latest research tends to support the view that simple legal contracts could be replaced by blockchain smart contracts, especially those regarding digital goods. For more specific insights into their legal context, I recommend that you read the relevant law dissertations on smart contracts in the References section. In the paragraphs that follow, we will seek to gain a broader understanding of smart contracts and, in particular, their role in the Ethereum blockchain.

What is a smart contract?

Here is an example of a smart contract:[15]

```solidity
1    // Version of Solidity compiler this program was written for
2    pragma solidity ^0.6.0;
3
4    // Our first contract is a faucet!
5    contract Faucet {
6        // Accept any incoming amount
7        receive () external payable {}
8
9        // Give out ether to anyone who asks
10       function withdraw(uint withdraw_amount) public {
11
12           // Limit withdrawal amount
13           require(withdraw_amount <= 100000000000000000);
14
15           // Send the amount to the address that requested it
16           msg.sender.transfer(withdraw_amount);
17       }
18   }
```

Even if you are not a coder or a software engineer, I bet you will have seen an example of the source code of a computer program somewhere before.

---

[15] Source:
github.com/ethereumbook/ethereumbook/blob/develop/code/Solidity/Faucet.sol

As you can see, a smart contract looks like exactly the same; for all intents and purposes, it is a computer program.

However, smart contracts work a little differently, thanks to two key intrinsic characteristics:

Immutability: Once deployed, the code of the smart contract cannot be changed. The concepts of ownership or rights permission do not apply; the only way to modify a smart contract is to deploy a new one.[16]

Determinism: The outcome of a smart contract is always the same. It is completely independent of the agent who activates the contract as well as any external conditions. Neither the blockchain state nor the network can interfere with the outcome of a contract.

As with any computer program, a smart contract can be built for virtually any purpose. However, its deployment in a blockchain means complying with specific requirements if it is to be executed properly. In turn, the platform on which it is deployed will ultimately influence the architecture of the performed contract.

Smart contracts and Bitcoin

Using the Bitcoin blockchain to store data unrelated to payments has been the subject of much debate. Many have tried to adapt the scripting language to exploit the system's security and resilience for applications such as notary services or proof-of-existence. After the introduction of the pay-to-script-hash and the return operator, a compromise was reached in the community so that, from early 2012, it was possible to execute smart contracts on the Bitcoin blockchain.

---

[16] Recently, some providers have introduced editing features to smart contracts but these are widely contentious due to their security implications.

For the sake of clarity, it is important to note that a smart contract cannot be directly stored on the Bitcoin blockchain. For this reason, many in the industry call them *bitcoin scripts*.

Whether we wish to call them smart contracts or bitcoin scripts, here are some of the most widely utilized:

Timelock—The simplest form of smart contract in the Bitcoin blockchain is called *timelock*. With timelocks, it is possible to add restrictions on transactions that only allow spending after a certain point in time. Many forms of sophisticated timelocks have been developed, also involving more than one transaction. Indeed, it is possible to link the execution of one transaction to another with a certain delay of time between the two. Timelocks have also enabled contracts such as promises of payment and installment plans.

Flow control—For those with limited coding literacy, flow control refers to the IF/THEN statements. Basically, flow control is a system that defines a preset transaction output based on unpredictable actions or events.

Here is an example of how flow control works:

IF user X initiates a transaction within the time T, **THEN** we have output A.

IF user X fails to initiate a transaction within the time T, **THEN** we have output B.

Flow control functions can be nested infinitely, so that the output of a previous transaction can also be the input of a subsequent transaction.

Here is another example of flow control scripts, this time with real goods:

Let's say that this book is sold in Bitcoin, and it is said that (**IF**) people buy this book within the first month, (**THEN**) they receive a 10% discount on the purchase price; otherwise, the book is charged at full price. The book is published on January 1 at the price of 1 BTC, and the last day to redeem the discount offer is January 31.

Those book-buyers who initiate the transaction before the 31ˢᵗ will trigger a smart contract that refunds the customer 10%, i.e., 0.1 BTC. Otherwise, the transaction is executed as normal. Since infinite other conditions may be added via flow control, let's add another hypothesis. We can add that if the refund is delayed by more than one day, a further 5% is discounted. So, if a customer purchases the book before January 31, a smart contract is triggered that refunds the 10%, but if the refund is only confirmed after 24 hours have passed, another transaction is initiated that reimburses an extra 5%.

Of course, the potential applications of the flow control function are infinite. Programmers know that flow controls also imply other operators, such as ENDIF or NOTIF. But a detailed explanation of operators is beyond the scope of this book.

Proof-of-existence: As discussed in the previous chapter, a block created on the chain bears some important characteristics. For it to be non-erasable and immutable, every block also contains a timestamp to facilitate exploration of the blockchain. A document added to the blockchain will then benefit from all these blockchain characteristics. First, it will be held forever on the blockchain.[17] Second, it cannot be forged by a malevolent agent. Third, it will have an exact timestamp of its creation. This feature, called *proof-of-existence*, is sought out as a sort of digital notary—to be implemented for documents with a legal value.

Colored coin: The purpose of the colored coin is to track real-world assets held by third parties and trade them through a certificate of ownership. Assets that are tradable in this system may include stocks, licenses, copyrights, oil, silver, land titles, automobiles, and so on. The word "colored" here comes from the idea of marking a note to represent something other than its nominal value. It is the equivalent of writing the following on a $10 bill: "Whoever owns this bill can redeem it for a wheel

---

[17] Depending on the blockchain, the document will mostly be stored in its hashed form.

of XYZ cheese." The bill has a nominal value of $10, but anyone who possesses this specific bill can also redeem a wheel of XYZ cheese.

The same premise applies to Bitcoin. A fraction of a Bitcoin can be marked (colored) with a message that links that amount to an asset, whether it is tangible or not. However, unlike simple Bitcoin transactions that can be auditable by anyone using an explorer, a colored coin can only be inspected using ad hoc software.

Although developers have exerted many efforts to adapt the Bitcoin blockchain to all sorts of smart contracts, apart from the transaction kind outlined above, others have proven complicated and cumbersome to implement. This is because the Bitcoin language is *Turing-incomplete.*

For non-insiders, this means that the Bitcoin language is intended to execute only a predetermined type of operations that, for Bitcoin in particular, is primarily concerned with payments. For other applications, the Bitcoin language is not developer-friendly. To further develop blockchain applications, developers must choose between building on top of the Bitcoin blockchain or creating a new one.

For this very reason, in 2013, a young programmer named Vitalik Buterin shared a new whitepaper outlining the idea of a Turing-complete, general-purpose blockchain. In 2015, Ethereum was launched.

The Ethereum blockchain

The founders of Ethereum set out to create a blockchain with no specific purpose, which could therefore be programmed for a wide variety of applications. The desired outcome was to deploy a platform in which developers could program their specific applications without the need to implement the underlying mechanisms of peer-to-peer, consensus algorithms, etc. This would result in a virtual machine, allowing developers to code their programs just as they would with regular virtual machines (e.g., Java virtual machines).

A complex and challenging project, the Ethereum blockchain had many phases of deployment. These phases served to shape and adapt the Ethereum blockchain to the evolving needs of the community. For example, although its original consensus mechanism was the proof-of-work (just like Bitcoin), Ethereum has now moved to a *proof-of-stake*.[18]

Ethereum and proof-of-stake

Although it has been argued that the proof-of-stake (PoS) constitutes an evolution of proof-of-work (PoW), this is not the case.

Unlike proof-of-work, proof-of-stake enables faster and cheaper transactions. Proof-of-stake affords those holding a stake in the currency the right to validate new blocks and earn rewards. Instead of investing in computing power and energy, miners on PoS blockchains take the name of *witnesses*.

Unlike miners, witnesses risk their stake of cryptocurrency in order to validate new blocks. Ideally, the system should be able to distinguish between rightful or malevolent transactions and thus reward or punish the corresponding witnesses. While there are many other currencies that use PoS (e.g., Tezos, Algorand) and different varieties of PoS (DPoS, LPoS), here I will only outline the one used on the Ethereum blockchain.

First, any would-be witness on the Ethereum blockchain must hold a minimum of 32 ETH.[19] Second, the person must be running a validator node. In itself, running a validator node is not particularly complex, nor does it require a specialized machine. However, the device must always be connected and running; if not, sanctions are imposed.

Although it is true that it is possible to stake with 32 ETH, in reality, it is also possible to participate in the staking process with a lower amount

---

[18] Ethereum is in the process of completing this transition at the time of this book's publication.

[19] ETH stands for Ether, which is the native cryptocurrency of the Ethereum blockchain.

thanks to the so-called "staking pools". Rewards obtained by staking pools are then distributed according to the staking amount minus service fees. However, as the transition to proof-of-stake is still under development, the exact rules and underlying mechanisms are still subject to change.

Significantly, it is a common opinion that—although the system is built to allow anyone to participate in the staking process—it is more likely that companies such as exchanges will have a predominant role in the process, since they can invest larger sums.

In the end, though, the most compelling advantage of PoS is that it requires only a negligible amount of energy consumption.

Gas and Turing-completeness

Turing-completeness is a feature that permits a machine to run any program. That being said, a Turing-complete machine is not necessarily more sophisticated than a Turing-incomplete one. In fact, the opposite holds true.

Building a Turing-incomplete machine means adding constraints to the plethora of possible instructions executed by the system. These restrictions are what make Bitcoin such an advanced platform.

There is, however, a problem to consider when thinking about machines in general. I think all of us, irrespective of technical expertise, have experienced a crash, blue screen, or hanging software on a computer or small appliance. The standard (and usually quite effective) approach is to reset or turn off the appliance; in the vast majority of cases, when the device has rebooted, the problem is solved. Even if the problem shows up again, it hardly bothers the user enough for them to want to understand its underlying cause.

Let's now try to contextualize the same problem with a public machine like Ethereum. As we know, blockchain cannot be turned off or rebooted, so any crash, loop, or blue screen cannot be resolved in the usual way.

Furthermore, if an operation proceeds in a loop, it will waste precious system resources, slowing down the entire platform. If more loops or halts are added, then the system can easily collapse. This is why the Bitcoin blockchain—in its Turing-incompleteness—only allows transactions that should not trigger system loops or crashes.

On the other hand, given that the original purpose and innovation of Ethereum was to be Turing-complete, an additional feature was needed that would encourage programmers to create safe and functional smart contracts. Fee payment alone cannot prevent users from creating bugged contracts or executing a malicious application with the sole purpose of slowing the system.

The solution to this issue arrived in the form of *gas*. Gas is a currency used on the Ethereum blockchain, which is paid for the execution of a smart contract. Different from Bitcoin, which is intended to be stored and transacted, the scope of gas is limited to executing transactions and smart contracts on the blockchain.

However, for those operations to be executed, a price must be paid. Obtaining gas to run a smart contract is simple and automatic. It is not possible to buy gas directly on an exchange; it is provided directly by the platform when executing smart contracts.

The native currency on the Ethereum blockchain is the ether. When users execute a smart contract, their ether is converted into gas and paid to the system. In other words, gas is the name for the equivalent of fees for Bitcoin transactions, but on the Ethereum blockchain.

The existence of fees makes it useful to run any type of smart contract. Even if the smart contract is bugged and goes into a loop executing continuous transactions, the machine will run it as long as there is enough ether in the contract's wallet. In this way, miners are also rewarded for faulty contracts. However, when the wallet is empty, the machine will stop executing the contract.

Smart contracts and EOAs

There are two types of addresses on the Ethereum Blockchain: smart contracts and *externally owned addresses* (EOAs).

EOAs are basically the same as Bitcoin addresses. They have private and public keys, and they can send and receive payments. The same rules apply, too: if the private key is lost, it can no longer be operated, and any funds stored in the address will be lost forever. The owner of the private key is the owner of the address.

Smart contract addresses, on the other hand, are not owned by anybody; they are self-owned. Contract addresses have no private keys, so there is no way to control them. Furthermore, the creator of a contract cannot be considered the owner, as once it is deployed, he will have no special rights over it.[20] The only way to modify a contract is to destroy and rebuild it.

It is important to note that, even if a contract is destroyed and no longer operable, the transaction history will remain forever embedded in the blockchain. This indelible transaction history constitutes an integral feature of smart contracts. Since smart contracts cannot be deleted and are always auditable (by anyone), it is understandable why there is so much hype around them in the legal system: they offer the potential of resolving disputes faster and more effectively.

The presence of two types of addresses on the Ethereum blockchain is not random. While it may appear as though smart contracts serve a utility function and EOAs and Ether were created for speculative purposes, this is not correct. The real reason why EOAs exist on the Ethereum blockchain is that smart contracts cannot self-execute. The only way to activate a smart contract is to send some gas from the EOA.

---

[20] However, if specified in the contract code, the owner may have the power to destroy the contract.

Finally, it is possible for a smart contract to execute another one, but the starting input should always come from an EOA. For example, gas can be sent to a contract that activates another one under certain conditions. Typically, the contract creator will fund the contract with some ether so that it essentially becomes "self-sufficient."

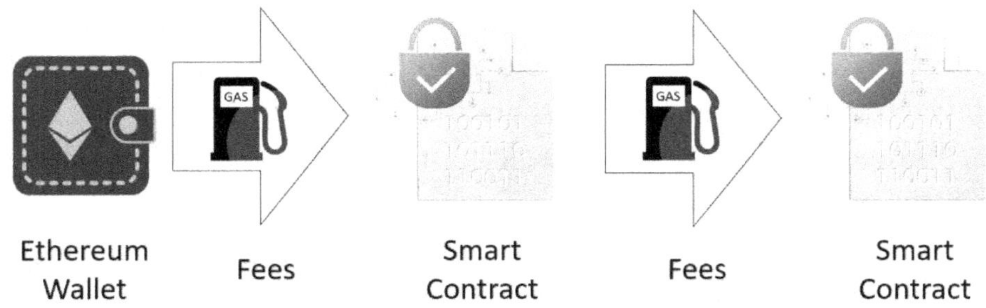

Examples of smart contracts

The most basic example of a smart contract is the *atomic swap*: the exchange of one cryptocurrency for another.

There are many possible reasons for exchanging cryptocurrencies. Perhaps we are no longer happy with those we have, or we are afraid of volatility, or we would like to invest in a new project.

Let's look at a scenario in which we are afraid of a market downturn and wish to exchange some volatile Ether (ETH) for more stable Tether (USD-T). (Tether is a stable coin that should always be exchanged at the price of $1; conversely, ether is extremely volatile). To exchange our currency, all we have to do is send the amount of ether we wish to convert to the smart contract address, pay the gas, wait for confirmation from the network, then wait for the contract to carry out the exchange.

CRYPTO SWAP

ETH

USD-T

But there is one crucial detail missing from this description of a smart contract: How does the smart contract know the exchange rate for the two cryptocurrencies involved?

The simple answer is that the smart contract does not know the exchange rate, because it is not a type of data elaborated by the blockchain. To recap, we know that, on the Bitcoin blockchain, this data comprises the addresses, the amount of currency transacted, and the timestamp. On Ethereum, we also have the smart contract code and output, which is registered forever on the chain. Therefore, unless the contract creator writes into the code the exchange rate (which would make no sense since it changes constantly), this data has to be fetched somewhere else.

As a result, smart contracts rely on third parties to fetch data from the external world. Usually, within the smart contract, the developer indicates the device or data source to query when the contract is executed.

These data sources are known as *oracles*.

Thanks to the oracles' data, smart contracts like the above-mentioned atomic swap can easily be executed.

The next two chapters provide an in-depth explanation of how oracles function and how they impact blockchain performance.

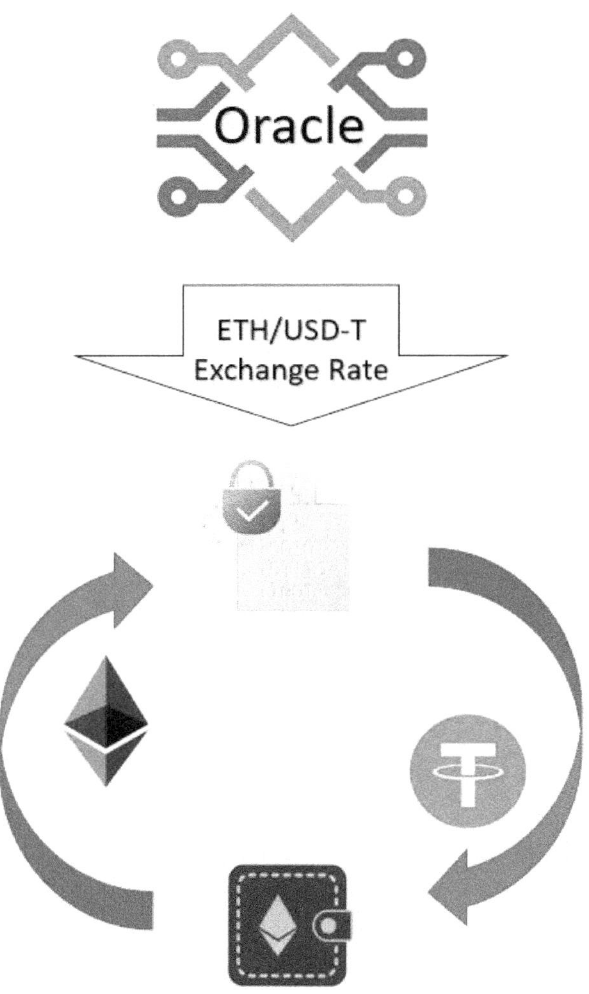

Chapter 3

The oracles

The term *oracle* comes from Greek mythology and refers to someone who is able to communicate directly with God and see the future. In ancient stories, when people lacked the necessary information to make decisions, they would turn to oracles for knowledge beyond their understanding. Decisions made with the help of oracles could also be justified as the will of a higher entity.

In the context of blockchain, oracles cannot open a communication channel between our world and the divine, but they do link two separate realms: the real world and the blockchain itself.

As seen in the previous chapter, oracles provide a smart contract with the ability to access data from sources outside the blockchain. In principle, blockchain computations and scripts can only involve data that already exists on the chain. This limit prevents the implementation of any type of application other than the simple transfer of currency and is based on the need to reach a decentralized consensus. Since every node must reach an agreement for the transaction to be confirmed, every actor needs to have all the required data at his disposal to verify its truthfulness. In public blockchains, moreover, their transparency allows anyone to audit the ledger and spot incorrect transactions; the addition of a block containing an erroneous transaction can be easily prevented.

On the contrary, when a transaction involves data from an external source, the other nodes of the chain cannot verify the given information. Since the data is unverifiable, there is no chance of reaching a decentralized consensus. Therefore, information from the real world should be sent by a third party whose reliability is indisputable for all nodes: the oracle.

Despite their classical Greek origins, blockchain oracles do not predict the future; instead, they retrieve relevant information from the past that allows a specific smart contract to be executed.

In essence, when other nodes have to approve a transaction, they take for granted that the oracle's data is true. Examples of data gathered by oracles include the following:

- Prices and exchange rates of real/crypto assets
- Static data (e.g., country codes)
- Dynamic data (e.g., time measurements)
- Geolocation and traceability information
- Weather conditions
- Political events
- Sporting events
- Lottery winners
- Natural disasters (and risk measurements)
- Accidents
- Events in other blockchains.

As shown in the previous chapter, exchange rates can be used to power atomic swap smart contracts. Dynamic data and geolocation can instead be exploited for the traceability of goods on the blockchain. Natural disasters and risk measurement can, on the other hand, enable smart contracts for insurance purposes. Intuitively, different data requires different oracle types.

Distinguishing oracles

Placement

Depending on 'where' they perform their assigned operations, the oracle can be classified as *on-chain* or *off-chain*.

On-chain oracles

On-chain oracles perform activities and computation directly on the blockchain. This means that executing their smart contract comes at a cost (in gas), and retrieved data is directly stored on the blockchain regardless of its final use.

Implementing on-chain oracles has both advantages and drawbacks. The benefits comprise transparency, integrity, and availability of data. Since the computation is directly performed on the blockchain, its content can be easily auditable by anyone if the blockchain is public, or by allowed people if the network is private. The retrieved data cannot be altered and will forever be accessible once stored on the blockchain. However, executing on-chain computation incurs fees that can skyrocket in networks like Ethereum during periods of congestion. Computation can also be sluggish since network resources are limited, and the user may end up storing data that is not used in the final contract.

Off-chain oracles

The term off-chain suggests that oracles sit somewhere outside the blockchain. In reality, their position could be the same as on-chain oracles. The key difference lies in how they run operations and upload outputs on the blockchain. In particular, off-chain oracles perform computations, draw data from the external world, and store it externally.

Unlike their on-chain equivalents, off-chain oracles help to distinguish data that serves the execution of contracts from data that is not useful for this purpose. As a result, only the data that serves the smart contract is uploaded on the blockchain and registered forever in the ledger. Unused data can then either be used at a later time or deleted.

Again, there are advantages and disadvantages to this kind of solution. First, the cost is definitely lower than on-chain. Although the running costs of the device are more or less the same, in the off-chain model, fees to execute the smart contracts are only paid when the oracle provides useful data. Furthermore, as the computation is run outside the chain, the oracle can benefit from faster and more efficient applications, unconstrained by the limits of the blockchain network. On the other hand, since all the data is not transferred to the blockchain, the off-chain suffers from a lack of transparency with regard to oracle activity.

Automation

Depending on the implemented hardware, the nature of the oracle, and the degree of automation, the following distinctions can be made.

Software oracles

Software oracles are primarily based on web application programming interfaces (APIs). For example, if the smart contract involves the refund of an outdoor gig ticket in case of a storm, the oracle can draw information from a weather forecasting website. As a website is a form of software, it will only transmit data based on information obtained elsewhere.

Typically, when a smart contract involving a software oracle is made, its data source is also underlined in the code. This approach is reasonably inexpensive and simple to implement. However, it is also easy to discern how it can fail.

In the example of a ticket reimbursement in case of bad weather, drawing information from a forecasting website may not be the best option; I'm sure we've all made plans based on the weather forecast only for the reality to prove the opposite. We may have decided not to go out due to a forecasted typhoon that never came or ended up trapped in a seaside resort sheltering from an unexpected downpour. Likewise, a weather forecast website cannot be expected to pinpoint the exact location of the event arena; rain in the surrounding area may end up passing the arena, leaving the event unaffected.

In smart contracts, on the other hand, the contract will be executed based on the source data, regardless of its truthfulness. However, it may still be advantageous to use software oracles because they are relatively inexpensive, fast, and yield a relative abundance of available data.

Web API   Blockchain

Hardware oracles

The role of a hardware oracle is to transmit data recorded on a hardware device securely. Unlike software oracles, hardware oracles are tangible entities like probes, sensors, radio-frequency identification (RFID) chips, meters, etc. For example, a hardware oracle can be a device used to check the temperature of a container.

Let's consider, for example, a covid-19 vaccine that must be kept at -80°C in transit. In this case, an oracle could be used to check the temperature of the delivery vehicle and to promptly communicate any changes or malfunctions in the refrigeration system.

Hardware oracles are particularly efficient since they can be placed precisely where they are needed. In the example of the ticket refund in case of rain, a sensor device could be placed in or near the arena and set up to communicate to the smart contract if it senses water on its surface. Unlike the forecast website, the sensor can respond immediately and independently in case of weather change, and whether the change is from good to bad or vice versa.

But just like software, hardware oracles are not 100% reliable. What if someone deliberately or inadvertently pours water on our sensor? It is unlikely that the sensor will be able to differentiate rain from the sky from water from a can: regardless of the true event, the sensor will transmit to the contract that "it's raining," influencing the outcome whether correctly or not.

Ultimately, if properly managed and supervised, hardware oracles are more efficient than software oracles, but they are also more expensive.

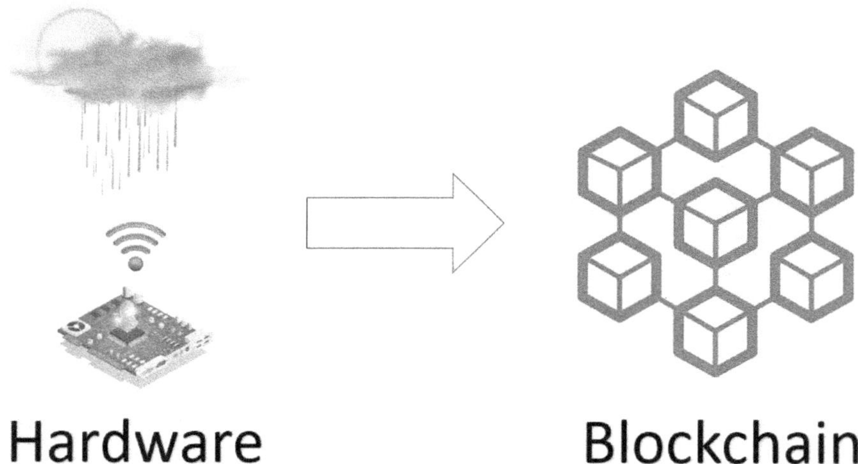

Human oracles

Intuitively, hardware and software oracles, being computer-based, can easily handle a considerable load of transactions.

Let's look at a sporting analogy. Suppose an events company that handles hundreds of football matches enables smart contracts to refund customers in full in case of adverse weather conditions. Even if thousands of matches are played at the same time, if the oracle draws its source data from the weather forecast website, it can simultaneously and effortlessly monitor the weather for all the cities and countries involved. Managing thousands of transactions is an ordinary task for a web API, so the oracle can handle all the requests.

In the case of hardware oracles, the only difference comes in the quantity of interfaces required to retrieve all the necessary data (i.e., the number of sensors needed at all the match-day stadia). However, as soon as all the sensors are placed, the smart contract can then efficiently and easily handle the data.

Let's now hypothesize that a human has to check and transfer all the source data manually to the oracle. This would be not only hard but also highly inefficient. Although humans can easily tell if it is raining or not, we can only handle a limited number of tasks at once. Furthermore, checking the weather in every stadium would require a substantial workforce, logistics, communication network, and so on.

However, there are cases in which hardware or software implementation cannot efficiently fetch the required data from the real world. Again, in the case of a football match, a sensor can easily determine whether it has started to rain, but will it also understand the outcome of the game? Can a sensor ever perceive the winner of a match or of an election?

For arbitrary data, then, software and hardware are unlikely to prove efficient. Humans, on the contrary, are perfectly capable of handling such a task. Properly skilled humans can also serve in specific fields where machines are still not programmed to perform. Evaluating a student, for example, is a task that is still mainly left to the appropriate personnel. If a smart contract involves the issuance of a certificate, it is the teacher who would have to testify to the successful acquisition of a learned skill.

Human oracles not only communicate with the blockchain but also constitute the source of its data. This is another key difference between human and artificial (hardware/software) oracles. With the latter, the data source can be easily distinguished from the device; these roles overlap in humans.

As for security, human oracles are mostly secure. Humans who serve as oracles have a private key that identifies them each time they access the blockchain. Of course, this key can be stolen, but the highest risks arise from human error or the deliberate upload of fraudulent data for personal gain. The transparency over oracle identity and reputation systems, however, are efficient methods to address these issues.

Activity

Oracles can also be distinguished based on the activity performed. Certainly, all oracles serve as a bridge between the blockchain and the real world, but since the flow of data is not unidirectional and is often not 'digested' in its original form, further distinction is required.

Computation oracles

Sometimes smart contracts need to not only gather the available data from the real world but also to perform certain computations. However, since computational network power is limited and costly, it will be nearly impossible to do all the on-chain calculations.

In these circumstances, oracles perform off-chain computations once they retrieve all the required data. The data used to run the smart contracts is then provided not directly from the real world but from the oracle that performed the computations.

To illustrate this, let's hypothesize that a smart contract triggers an indemnity to a set of farmers in case a storm destroys the harvest. The contract is based on the type of disaster, the area of the terrain affected, and the expected revenues. While these data points are necessary to evaluate the subsidy entity, they do not constitute the data required for the contract. The oracle must then elaborate on the acquired data and compute a sum to be sent to each individual farmer. Finally, the output of the computation constitutes the data submitted to the contract.

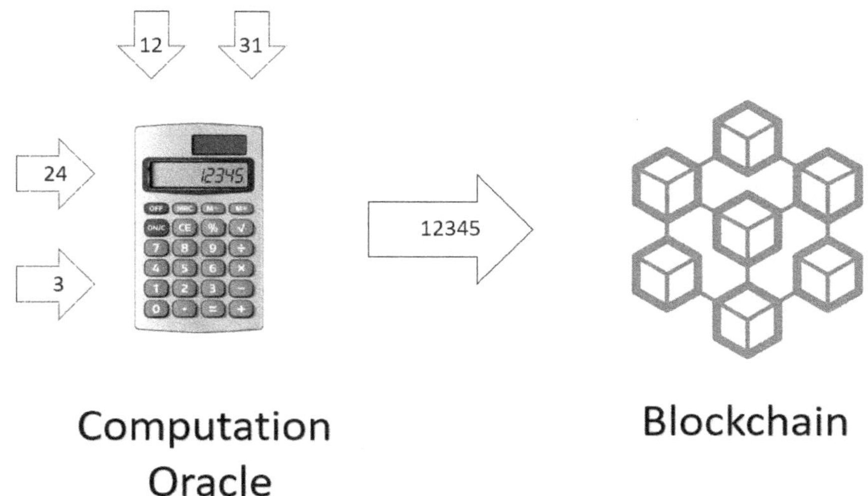

Computation Oracle

Blockchain

Inbound oracles

Inbound oracles are the most common. The word *inbound* refers to the flow of data from the real world into the blockchain. Most of the examples mentioned above are inbound oracles, including temperature sensors, weather forecasts, and exchange rate services.

Outbound oracles

Alternatively, outbound oracles appear in circumstances where data from the blockchain is utilized to influence real-world events. These types of contracts are rarely heard about, however, because making inbound transactions is already a complex enough process. As such, outbound transactions remain underdeveloped.

To have a clearer idea of how an outbound oracle works, it is helpful to imagine a future in which smart contracts are able to manage holiday homes autonomously. If we wish to rent such a property, we are required to send a certain sum of money to the proprietary wallet. Once this sum is safely deposited, the smart contract unlocks the house's door. In this smart lock example, the flow of data starts inside the blockchain and passes into the real world. (As far as I know, such an application does not yet exist, but it is useful for illustrative purposes.)

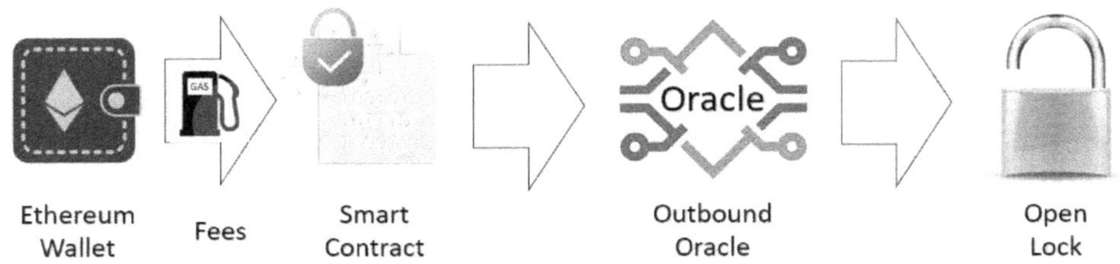

Atypical oracles

Atypical oracles are those that follow unique patterns and include features that differ from the standard types. They emerge from circumstances in which public repositories do not provide all the requirements for a specific contract, and new types need to be created.

Contract-specific oracles

As the name suggests, contract-specific oracles are built specifically for smart contracts.

If we want to build multiple smart contracts, we must also write as many oracles as there are contracts. This is a definite inconvenience, especially for smart contracts that involve agreements of low value. It is therefore desirable for smart contracts to feature a certain degree of customization.

Similarly, having ad hoc oracles means writing them from scratch so that any contract requirements can be included. Again, this is not the most appropriate type for ordinary contracts since it is costly and time-consuming. An atypical example would be an insurance policy for a celebrity that covers atypical things like hair or nails against unpredictable events. To be able to issue such an atypical insurance policy, the insurer would have to write ad hoc oracles and smart contracts.

Consensus-based oracles

If the availability of data allows it, multiple oracles can be queried for a single request. If the smart contract involves the exchange rate of a currency, for instance, it is possible to query more than one web API to verify the fetched data. Equally, when the contract involves a consistent amount of money or it has a legal value, it makes sense to query more than one oracle to ensure that the retrieved data is appropriate for the contract.

There is no prescription for the perfect number of oracles or efficiently proven consensus models. Some contracts query two oracles, while others query more than 20. The outcome that is considered correct can be a mean between oracles or the value returned by the majority.

While there are no rules on this point, the more oracles are involved, the more costly the contract will be. It is also probable that the more complex the consensus mechanism, the slower the contract will be executed.

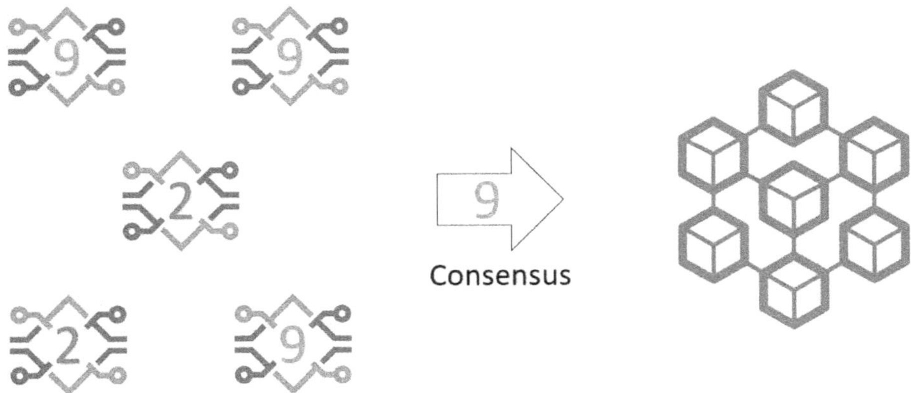

Control

Depending on the degree of control that the smart contract owner has on the oracle, it is possible to distinguish between centralized and decentralized. Unlike the previous distinction based on the consensus model, the following does not exclusively refer to their number.

Centralized Oracles

Regardless of their number, oracles are considered centralized when their position and functionality are controlled by a single entity.

There are certain conditions in which this is to be preferred. If, for example, oracles detect movement under the sea in a protected bay, they will probably all be under the control of the local coastguard. This constitutes not a limit but a guarantee that the data collected is used for the right purpose.

Oracles can also be centralized by nature. Imagine a human oracle who is, for example, a Nobel Prize winner and the only keeper of a particular scientific discovery. If this person's knowledge has to be uploaded to the blockchain, he or she is the only one able (and allowed) to do so.

Of course, there are scenarios in which centralized oracles are not desirable. Let's take the case of a mineral water producer that wishes to certify, using blockchain, that its water does not come from a polluted area. The company provides a QR code that shows the flow of the water before it is sold at the supermarket. To do so, they install sensors that transmit the relevant blockchain data on the position of water, its flow rate in gallons per hour, and possibly chemical data about its mineral content. In this case, since the company installed the oracles, it does not matter if there are two or 2,000 sensors in the system, because they are centralized under the control of the same entity. However, if the motive here is to prove that the water is safe, this is not the right approach. Intuitively, the water producer can say whatever they want from these oracles. On the other hand, if implementing the blockchain is for internal audit purposes (e.g., to check that the course of water has not been altered), it makes sense to use centralized oracles. As the company will directly manage the data, they will have no reason to alter it.

Decentralized Oracles

Decentralized oracles are not necessarily consensus oracles; likewise, consensus oracles are not always decentralized.

I will try to be as precise as possible on this point since it is not a straightforward one. Say we have a company that wants to detect the acidity of a certain stretch of terrain. They may decide to place more than one sensor in the ground and gather the relevant data from each of them. If there are 10 sensors, the company may base its analyses on the value provided by the majority. In this case, the 10 devices are centralized, consensus-based oracles; although we have multiple oracles, they all belong to the same entity.

By contrast, decentralization refers to the degree of direct control that the contract creator (or user) has over the oracle. In the mineral water example above, we hypothesized that the company was responsible for installing all the oracles. Instead, let's suppose that, for water traceability, the company relies on oracles placed by other entities (e.g., forestry service, city council, university researchers) for different purposes. Now, the motive of proving the genuine quality of the water makes more sense, since the likelihood that the company could wield influence over government, municipal, or university research sensors is low.

The condition of low or no control over oracles, then, is what makes them decentralized. Surprisingly, having just one oracle does not imply that it is also centralized. This is, of course, a rather more controversial condition.

Consider the case of a company that creates a smart contract that requires at least one oracle to operate. Let's say that the company cannot place the oracle because of a conflict of interest or because it cannot access the data source directly; it may instead rely on a platform whereby the fastest oracle provides information every time it is needed. A single oracle will always provide the data, but it will probably be different every time. In that sense, even when fetching data from a single source, we may consider the system decentralized.

Closing remarks

Oracles are specialized devices that serve as a communication channel between the blockchain and the real world. Without their intervention, it would be almost impossible to implement smart contracts. Depending on the smart contracts and the specific sectors involved, different types of oracles can be implemented, each with its own strengths and limitations.

Ultimately, the implementation of the oracles on the blockchain has received widespread criticism from experts in the field due to its implications for blockchain reliability. This issue—better known as *the oracle problem*—will be extensively discussed in the next chapter.

Takeaway: Oracles fall into different categories. A specific oracle can be, for example, off-chain, centralized, consensus-based, and software-based.

Chapter 4

Understanding the oracle problem

The oracle problem is by no means a new concept in the field of information technology (IT). Before the advent of blockchains, oracles were known as entities used to verify the correct execution of test applications. Many researchers realized, however, that when oracles could not operate in a condition of complete automation, serious problems could arise. If oracles are not automated, an agent intervention is needed to determine whether the observed application's behavior is correct or not. Since human discretion is unable to foresee all possible outcomes, the uncertainty surrounding the feedback provided is known as *the oracle problem.*

In the field of blockchains, the oracle problem is indeed related to the technical reliability of oracles, but it also concerns their trustworthiness. The writer and web developer Brian Curran has defined the oracle problem as *"the security, authenticity, and trust conflict between third-party oracles and the trustless execution of smart contracts.*[21]*"* While this is not the only definition available, it does succinctly outline the concept.

The first appearance of the construct can probably be traced to a Reddit post by a user named 'Dalovindj.' The developer realized that, when executing an application on the Bitcoin blockchain regarding crowdfunding or gambling, verifying the reliability of extrinsic information without altering the consensus mechanism proved a difficult task: *"I think of it as 'The Oracle Problem.'"*[22]

---

[21] Source: https://blockonomi.com/oracles-guide
[22] Source: https://www.reddit.com/r/Bitcoin/comments/2p78kd/the_oracle_problem/

The foundation of the oracle problem lies in the apparent discrepancy of intent and capabilities between blockchains and oracles. On the one hand, blockchain is celebrated because it can remove the single point of failure and create an environment in which trust is not required. On the other hand, oracles are often centralized entities whose trustworthiness is paramount.

Whenever they use blockchain, people know that they can count on the immutability, security, transparency, and trustworthiness of data, but these features are no longer guaranteed if the blockchain utilizes oracles. In the same way that the resistance of a chain is based on its weakest link, in the case of blockchain applications, the weakest link is the oracle.

In a recent talk[23], Andreas Antonopoulos has explained that blockchain applications that rely on oracles may fail in two ways. First, even if the oracle is trusted and cannot be compromised, there is still a chance that the data on which it is working has been altered. In turn, although the device itself is trustworthy, it will feed untrue data into the smart contracts. Second, if the data are trusted and verified, the oracle may fail to operate on the smart contract correctly due to either malfunction or deliberate tampering. Data implementation into the blockchain could also jeopardize users' trust that blockchains are more reliable than legacy systems.

In another engaging talk on the oracle problem,[24] Paul Sztorc has discussed the likelihood of an oracle being deliberately altered. Sztorc argues that the importance and value of the smart contract are the key factors here.

In economics, we often refer to equilibrium theory to explain the relationship between incentives and behavior. The takeaway from Sztorc's

---

[23] Andreas M. Antonopoulos, "The Killer App: Bananas on the Blockchain?" https://aantonop.com/the-killer-app-bananas-on-the-blockchain/.

[24] Paul Sztorc, "Blockchain: The Oracle Problems," InfoQ, June 29, 2017, https://www.infoq.com/presentations/blockchain-oracle-problems/.

talk is that the higher the value of the smart contract, the higher the incentive for the system to be compromised.

Let's consider the example of an automated betting market prediction platform. The blockchain is unable to see what happens in the real world, so it relies on oracles to fetch the relevant data, including the outcomes of sporting events. In the case of small bets, sabotaging the oracles to win the pot would compromise the credibility of the platform and eventually lead to shut-down. In other words, the deterrent of losing future earnings should be sufficient to prevent malevolent behavior.

However, if by chance the pool of bets becomes so large that altering the results would mean receiving an unprecedented payout, the situation is different. The risk of closing down the platform may not counterbalance the potential earnings from the data tampering, so the deterrent effect is lost.

Once a lie is added to the chain, it will remain immutable and transparent. In IT, the expression *"garbage in, garbage out"* is often used to highlight the strict dependence of an application's reliability on its inputs. Thus, if smart contracts perform badly or produce an unwanted outcome, the reason is more likely to be the source data provided than a network malfunction.

Smart contract outcomes are not the only kind of transactions affected by the oracle problem. Attaching real-world assets (fruit, cars, houses) to the blockchain also involves the use of oracles. Of course, the ownership and handling of tangible assets are regulated by the relevant jurisdiction or governing body. This means that another entity is predominant in the smart contract; executing the contract therefore presupposes trust not only in the smart contract, but in the regulatory body as well.

Let's return to the holiday home example discussed in the previous chapter. Once the right money is deposited in the right wallet, the code will execute the smart contract, opening the smart lock and allowing the customer access to the property. Upon execution of the contract, the role of the blockchain is established: it writes on the ledger that the right of occupancy belongs to someone else from a certain point in time. Then, if properly coded, it can also enable the lock to be opened by the renter. However, the blockchain and the smart contract will have no bearing on real-world incidents that may impact the letting process. The previous guests may refuse to leave the apartment on time or tamper with the smart lock so they are still able to enter the property. In other words, the blockchain has no means to guarantee that the written event corresponds to what happens in the real world.

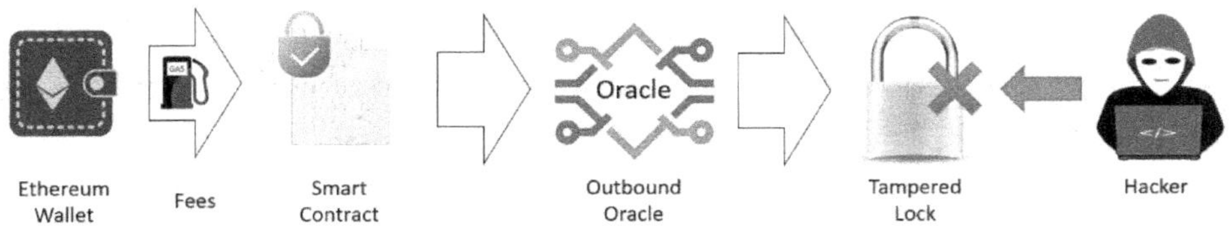

In the absence of an external authority that supervises the smart contract and intervenes in case someone prevents its correct execution, system reliability cannot be guaranteed.

However, the need to trust an entity 'above' the smart contract and the oracle removes the *killer feature* of trustless blockchain applications. If a multitude of other entities need to be trusted for a blockchain application to run effectively, the very use of blockchain is brought into question. And if blockchain has been proposed as a system to effectively manage contracts and properties in countries where institutions are untrustworthy or corrupted, how can they be a viable solution if they are reliant on a third-party authority?

Consequences of the oracle problem

In 2017, a Master's student named Alexander Egberts investigated the drawbacks of the implementation of oracles and its impact on the reliability of smart contracts—describing oracles as *"two steps back from decentralization."* I strongly believe that Egberts's contribution has revealed certain fundamental aspects of smart contracts, which were widely neglected up to this point. Below, I will briefly discuss some of Egberts's claims.

Decreasing security

Think of a platform as a house and its access portals as the doors and windows. The more doors and windows the house has, the greater its exposure to intrusion. If a house only has a front door, installing a security camera and a reinforced gate may be enough to prevent intruders from gaining access. But if the house has three doors, plus a garage entrance connected to the inside of the house, and a series of balconies directly over the road, deploying an effective security system is far more complex.

For IT applications, the mechanism is exactly the same. The more access software has, the more security weaknesses it will face. Therefore, adding a communication channel to the blockchain will inevitably increase its exposure to security threats. On the one hand, then, having a secure oracle is preferable to a non-secure oracle; on the other hand, any transaction made without an oracle will always be more *reliable* than a transaction determined with them.

Impact: Oracles reduce the security of blockchain applications.

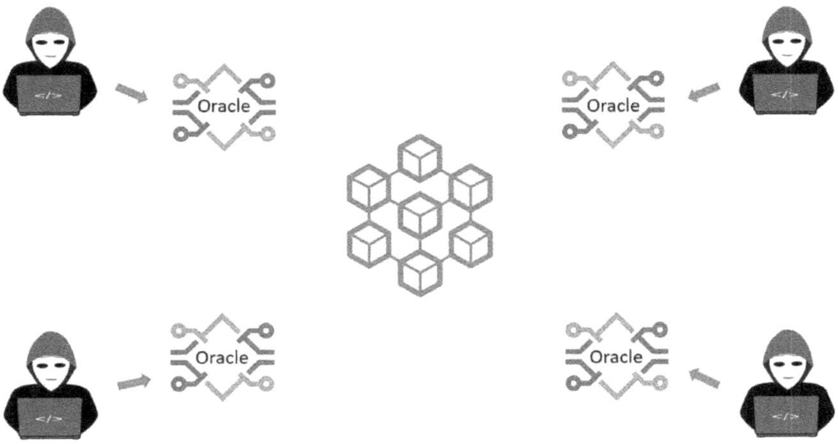

Reintroducing the single point of failure

As explained in Chapter 1, the power of the blockchain lies in its elimination of the single point of failure, thanks to the consensus mechanism. This allows Bitcoin, for example, to function without the help or supervision of an external authority. Most importantly, the system cannot be altered or destroyed since all the copies of the ledger are master copies. Even if hundreds of copies are destroyed or altered, the remaining 'healthy' ones ensure the system's survival. Equally, if blockchain nodes provide data that has been forged, the platform can easily spot the impairment and switch allegiance to the majority of 'honest' nodes.

Oracles, on the other hand, are centralized entities and, even if they are distributed, they are still of an exiguous number. Damaging oracles will eventually alter smart contracts. Furthermore, if fake data is provided, the blockchain is powerless to prevent its registration in the system.

Impact: Using oracles inevitably undermines blockchain resilience and trustworthiness.

The incentive to cheat

As seen in Chapter 1, opportunities to cheat on the Bitcoin blockchain are extremely rare. Trying to perform an attack would, in any case, require an extraordinary amount of power, and success is not guaranteed. The wider the network, the harder any attempt to alter the ledger becomes. Cheating the Bitcoin blockchain would also demand a substantial sum of money to be spent in return for only a meager chance of success.

Knowing how hard it is to alter a system serves as a deterrent to malevolent parties and gives the reassurance of reliability to its users. In the case of oracles, however, it is definitely possible to shut down the oracles serving a smart contract and to alter the data they fetch, incentivizing attempts to breach system security. In turn, the understanding that oracles can be sabotaged harms user perceptions of system stability.

Impact: The use of oracles eventually increases the incentive to cheat on the blockchain.

Reintroducing trust

On a philosophical level, exploring the concept of trust is a tricky prospect. Trust is a more social concern than a technical one. Indeed, the oracle problem has often been described as a "social problem."

My preferred definition comes from Mayer, Davis, and Schoorman,[25] who state that **trust comprises the willingness to be vulnerable given a positive expectation of the other party**. Basically, trusting somebody means that (in our eyes) they will not cheat. As a result, we may lower our defenses and demand less information when interacting with them. On the flipside, of course, the trusted party may exploit this relationship to do harm. Yet if they have no means to harm us, we cannot tell if we really trust them.

In the context of blockchains, there is nothing to trust because the system is created to be independent and efficient. When you throw something out of the window, you do not have to trust in fate or destiny that the object will fall to the ground. In a blockchain environment, transactions will be processed while new blocks are added; we just know they will.

When considering blockchain applications involving oracles, however, the situation changes. We do not know if the oracles have been tampered with or if the source data is collected correctly. Similarly, we do not know if the smart contract is well-programmed or if the selected oracle is colluding with the contract owner for its own self-interest. Since these elements are all unknown and the oracle is in the best position to harm users, we must

---

[25] Roger Mayer, James Davis, and David Schoorman, "An Integrative Model of Organizational Trust," *Academy of Management Review*, 20, no. 3 (1995): 709–34, https://www.jstor.org/stable/258792.

place a considerable degree of trust in the system—and the oracles especially.

Impact: The implementation of oracles reintroduces the concept of trust in the blockchain.

The risk of trust oligopolies

The advantage of creating a blockchain version of current applications mainly revolves around reducing transaction costs.

Whenever we interact with someone for the first time, we uphold a certain degree of suspicion that helps us to prevent any future problems. But this mechanism comes at a relatively high cost.

For example, if we manage a company and an unknown supplier offers their products to us for the first time, it is unlikely that we will treat them in the same way as our regular suppliers. We may try an initial small sample of products, paying a higher price compared to bulk ordering. We may even provide some assurances that, if everything goes right, we will renew the supplier contract. Over time, with no inconvenience to ourselves, we could choose to place larger orders with lower or no insurance policies, thereby reducing our costs considerably.

Clearly, from the first interaction, we committed to certain expenses that we would have avoided if we had trusted the new supplier. In the same way, blockchain implementation should reduce the costs incurred if we interact with someone we do not already know.

The problem with blockchain, however, is that it relies on a limited number of centralized entities: the oracles. Moving applications to the blockchain would mean entrusting entire sectors to a select few oracles that are trusted by definition, not by actual practice. There is also the chance that a small enclave of oracles could gain control over industries that are usually characterized by a far greater number of actors. This centralization of power may give birth to *trust oligopolies*, which are far more dangerous than untrusted environments.

A system that is trusted by definition alone could ultimately jeopardize the standard mechanisms that customers impose to defend themselves from being ripped off. Trust oligopolies could easily exploit this predetermined level of trust for their own ends.

Impact: Regardless of type, the implementation of oracles triggers the centralization of trust.

Closing remarks

The oracle problem is a controversial subject with both technical and social aspects. Many projects have claimed to solve the oracle problem, but the majority only address the former and completely overlook the latter. Past research has endeavored to create a system of oracles that respond to the oracle problem from both a social and a technical point of view—building what is known as a *trust model*. Unfortunately, to date, projects that implement a compelling trust model remain scarce. These projects are the subject of discussion in the next chapter.

Chapter 5

Oracle providers

Having explored the role of oracles and the implications of the oracle problem, it is worth looking at how some companies have tried to address the problem and the challenges they have encountered along the way. This chapter examines some of the best-known cases, outlining their respective strengths and weaknesses.

As a researcher in the field, I have no contacts or partnerships with these companies; my sole motive for presenting real companies here is to explain how the oracle problem is currently being handled. Such an overview of companies providing oracle services is crucial to explaining how they promote decentralized trust. Furthermore, my choice of companies should not signal preference in any way. The decisions were made purely based on the availability of related information and the discrepancies between each company's approach.

In the following sections, I will first describe the driving purpose and innovation of each company involved, as well as the benefits and drawbacks of their approach, with the aim of being as non-technical as possible.

Augur

According to the Augur whitepaper[26], "*Augur is a trustless, decentralized oracle and prediction market platform.*" Put simply, Augur is an online platform that allows users to bet on any event[27].

Initially, Augur was designed to be an extension of Bitcoin and operated on the basis of Bitcoin scripts. Later, due to the versatility of the Ethereum Virtual Machine (EVM), Augur switched to the Ethereum smart contract-based architecture. The innovative part of the system is that it is entirely decentralized, so there is no central authority that supervises the event and settles the outcomes.

As you can imagine, the absence of authority implies some mechanism that can decide an event outcome's trustworthiness and resolve any disputes that may arise. But before we can understand how the Augur oracle works, it is best to consider how the Augur platform operates.

Unlike any other betting platform (like a traditional bookmaker) that offers a broad range of predetermined events to bet on, the Augur platform has no event offered by the developer. Anyone can create a "market," which is an event on which anyone can bet. Augur's own developers ensure that the system is secure and bug-free, and the platform operates according to a predetermined set of operations called *creation–trading–reporting–settlement*.

Here is the Augur market creation interface for a sporting event. Of course, the interface changes slightly depending on the type of event.

---

[26] Source: https://augur.net/.
[27] Of which results can be publicly auditable.

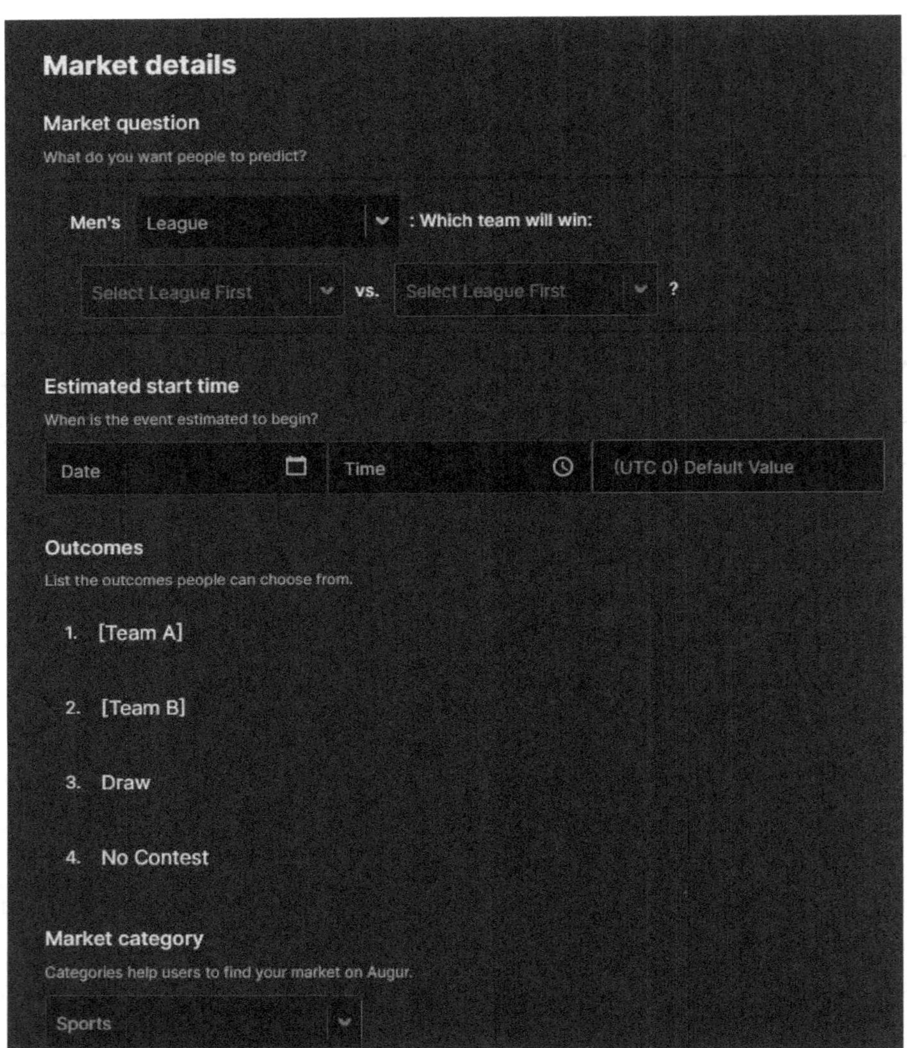

After a detailed description of the event type, there is another space to complete with event information, which would typically include the event's resolution, the timing of the event, and potential mitigating circumstances that would lead to the event being postponed or canceled.

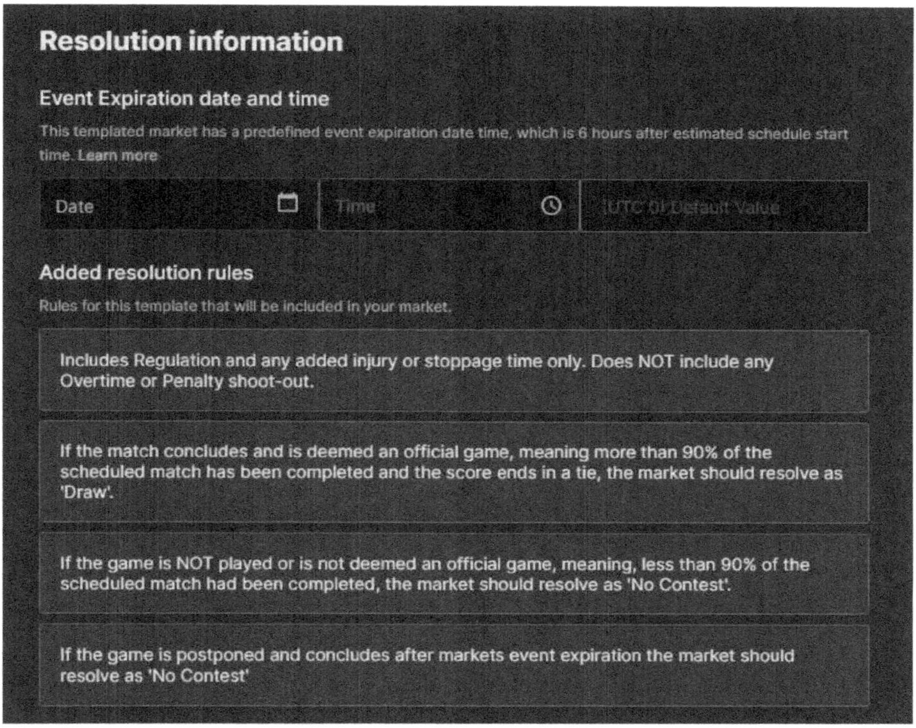

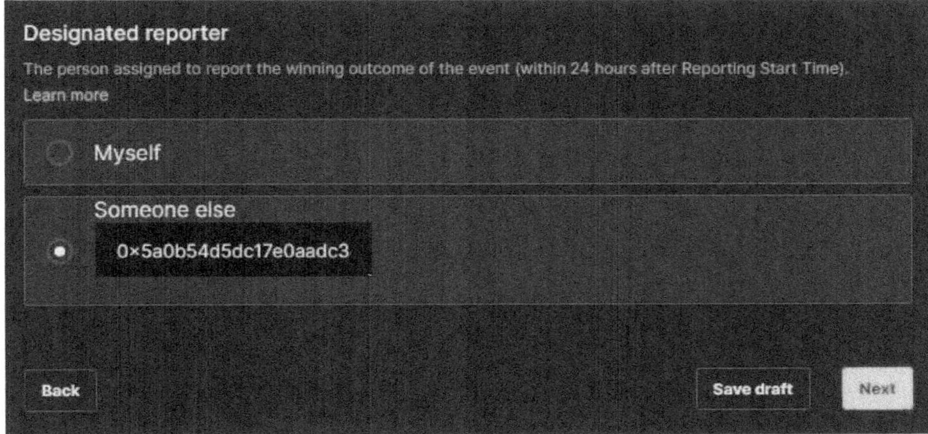

Finally, there is a box in which the market creator can indicate the *designated reporter* (i.e., the oracle). The Augur oracle then has the task of communicating the outcome of the event to the platform. In this particular case, the oracle could be the creator or another source of his choosing.

Here, the fact that the market creator can act as an oracle (or is allowed to choose a trusted source) may give the impression that the communication channel between the real world and the blockchain is centralized and unquestionable. However, Augur claims to be a decentralized oracle and goes to great lengths to explain how and why they aim to reach this status.

If the Augur platform response to the oracle problem is to divide its operation into creation–trading–reporting–settlement, the reporting phase will be the longest and most complex of the four.

The following figure summarizes this process:[28]

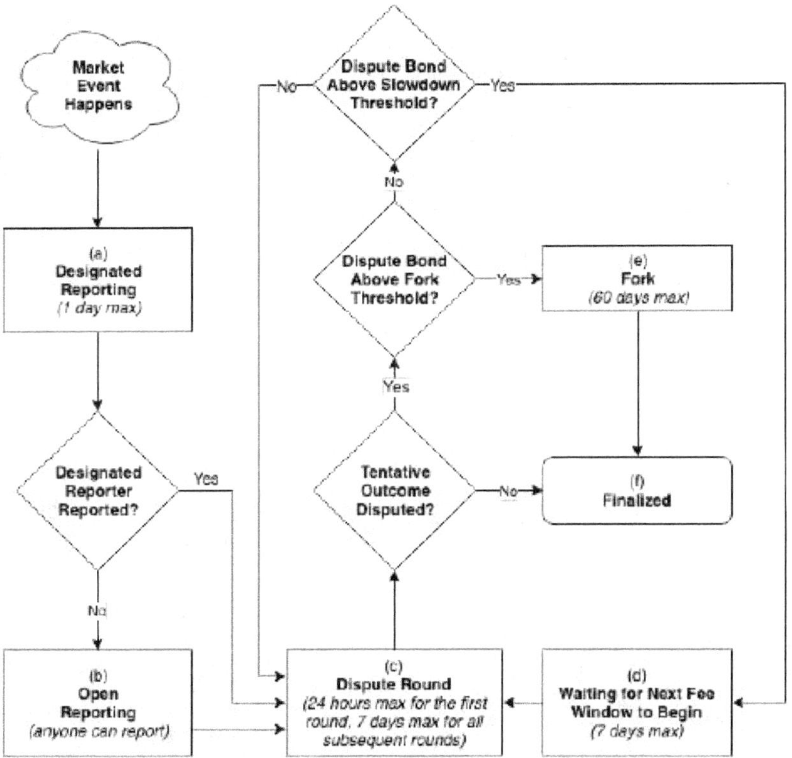

---

28 Source: https://augur.net/whitepaper.pdf.

Significantly, there is also a *pre-reporting* phase that occurs before the event and in conjunction with the trading phase. In this period, people may still bet on the outcome of the event (just like the roulette table, where players can still place bets while the roulette wheel is spinning).

Once the event has passed, the trading phase ends and the reporting phase begins. This is the moment at which the oracle communicates (or should communicate) the outcome of the event to the blockchain. If the oracle fails to communicate the outcome within 24 hours, an open reporting phase begins, in which anyone aware of the results can communicate them to the blockchain. Whether the results come from the 'original' oracle or an open oracle, a critical phase called the *dispute round* then begins.

During the dispute round, the tentative event outcome is made public, and other oracles are able to propose a different result if they think the event transpired differently. If the majority of oracles are in favor of the tentative outcome, then the dispute round ends, and the settlement phase starts. Otherwise, a new tentative outcome is submitted, and another dispute round starts; it is only once the majority of oracles agree that a tentative outcome is confirmed and the dispute round ends.

Augur is supported by an intriguing incentive mechanism for oracles to be trustworthy and cooperate with the platform.

First, oracles who participate in the platform receive fees based on the market size and their contribution. Second, oracles who successfully prevent an untrue outcome from being settled receive a 40% return on their investment. This means that subverting an unwanted outcome is considered more important than simply operating honestly on the platform. And, of course, the motivation is clear: if a false outcome is accepted and settled on the Augur platform, the whole system fails. Thus, preventing a false outcome from reaching settlement is understandably the most rewarded action for oracles.

Augur also features a last-resort mechanism called "the fork" to settle dispute rounds that fail to agree on an event's true outcome. Without going into too much detail of what is a very technical operation, during the fork, the system is split into two. Oracles then need to decide on which platform they wish to remain. Each platform represents a different outcome, and if the oracles choose the platform corresponding to the false event, all their money will lose its value. This perceived threat is deemed sufficient to force all the oracles to choose the platform that corresponds to the true outcome.

Drawbacks

1) Augur is an oracle based on the wisdom of the crowd, i.e., it can only reach a consensus for events whose outcomes are publicly accessible. The Augur team has stated that, if an event's outcome is non-public, the corresponding event should be marked as "invalid." This type of oracle cannot therefore be applied to private events or events whose outcomes are not "straightforward." (i.e., they cannot be determined objectively)

2) In the case of an event whose result is not straightforward, the outcome will be different depending on the people involved. For such subjective outcomes, "truth" cannot be unilateral. Even splitting the platform with a fork will divide the oracles according to what they perceive to be true. By doing so, none of the resulting platforms will lose the value of their currency and will continue existing as *parallel universes*.

3) The Augur solution to the oracle problem is based on a game-theoretical approach, which therefore implies rationality[29]. Of course, errors are expected and addressed in the dispute round, but irrational behavior is "non-solvable." Granted, oracles are

---

[29] The game theory is the study of mathematical models of strategic interaction among rational decision-makers. Source: Myerson, Roger B. (1991). Game Theory: Analysis of Conflict, Harvard University Press, p. 1

incentivized to be trustworthy as they receive a return on their investment, but what happens if they do not care? If oracles begin acting irrationally, the platform's equilibrium may be disrupted.

4) Augur uses a native token called REP (Reputation). It serves as an incentive and a deterrent to attackers who wish to feed false information into the blockchain. The value of the token is transmitted to the platform through third-party oracles. Therefore, we can assume that the whole system of trust is also dependent on the trustworthiness of those oracles, whose role and operability are beyond the control of the Augur team. However, Augur has recognized the significance of this limitation and is planning to cut this dependency in due course.

5) Augur runs the risk of exploitation by third parties. Since Augur oracles are compensated for their work (albeit only at a low level), certain fees are deducted from the prize pool. Another platform could then propose the same market and exploit Augur's own oracles for the outcomes while offering a better fee/prize share. Although Augur is unable to prevent this activity, at present, no such competitors have been identified.

6) Although Augur's solution to the oracle problem is both attractive and potent, it cannot be implemented on other projects, since it is only available on the Augur platform.

Chainlink

The Chainlink whitepaper[30] gives no clear definition of their service, but based on their commentary, we can define it as an *"all-purpose oracle intermediary platform"*.

Chainlink does not offer an oracle service directly; instead, it provides an intermediation service between application providers and data providers (oracles). The Chainlink case is important to consider because it illustrates how an intermediary platform has tried to resolve the oracle problem.

For the sake of clarity, I will briefly outline how the Chainlink platform operates.

The Chainlink team states that the platform is appropriate for a wide range of services, including securities, insurance, and trade finance. At the moment, they do not seem to be targeting any specific sector; their aim is to cover all potential markets. They also declare that, despite being built initially on Ethereum, they plan to reach all possible smart contracts on other networks.

We know that blockchain software developers need external data to operate their smart contracts. They will then need oracles to provide this data, and they are willing to pay for it. On the other side of the equation, there are services that provide secure data at a certain price. Under these circumstances, the role of Chainlink is pretty straightforward: as with any intermediary, it helps those two groups connect and helps resolve any disputes as they arise.

Through Chainlink, users can select the best oracle to fit their service from the providers available. When a user browses the oracle list, he or she can also see the oracle's historical data, such as timely performance and reputation. If the user's requests are dynamic and cannot be matched

---

[30] Source: https://chain.link/.

manually, Chainlink also offers an order-matching system. Based on the request (data needed/price offered), the system will automatically allocate all the relevant offers. Alternatively, Chainlink can also provide users with a selection of oracles that best match their needs. The final decision is left to the user.

Once definitive oracles are selected, Chainlink then registers the contract's data and updates the oracle's information with data on timeliness and reliability. After this data transfer, the service settles the payment according to the respective bids and offers.

In terms of user benefits, the proposed Chainlink model prioritizes three desired characteristics of oracles: the CIA triad of confidentiality, integrity, and availability.

Confidentiality—When users require data from oracles, they may need data to be confidential. Although blockchain platform transparency suggests that any data should be public, sensitive information such as personal user data should be kept private. Confidentiality also prevents the so-called *freeloading attack*, whereby an oracle exploits the transparency of data provided by other oracles to offer the same data at a lower price, pushing out trustworthy market oracles and disrupting the whole system's reliability.

To address this problem and to offer a confidentiality feature to its clients, Chainlink has implemented an *off-chain aggregation* (OCA) contract solution. Rather than committing to an answer on the blockchain, the Chainlink platform receives encrypted off-chain answers from oracles. Since these responses are encrypted, other oracles cannot copy data and hence cannot carry out freeloading attacks. Only once the match between bid and offer is settled is the answer revealed. This is also particularly useful in reducing the cost of an aggregate answer by multiple oracles: since every transaction on a public blockchain is costly, maintaining a decentralized on-chain system would be prohibitively so.

Integrity—This feature requires user data to be consistently trustworthy. Certainly, the notion of a perfectly trusted third party is something of an abstraction; no source can always be trusted. Even if someone is committed to telling the truth, he or she may still inadvertently provide faulty data.

Chainlink points to decentralization and trusted hardware as its solutions to the integrity problem.

The decentralization of response is made possible by having multiple oracles replying to one answer, so that even if a trusted oracle makes a mistake, as the number of oracles increases, the chance of committing erroneous data is low. In the end, given that faulty oracles (F) are far fewer than the total number of oracles (N), having more oracles boosts the reliability of the final answer.

When running properly, the Chainlink system should work according to the following scheme:[31]

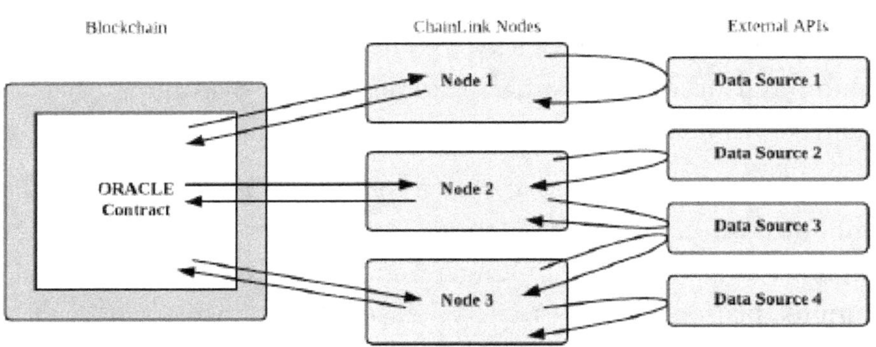

Having trusted hardware operating as oracles is another desirable condition that is obtainable in the long term. Trusted hardware reduces the chance of collecting inaccurate data. Moreover, long-term cooperation with a trusted hardware oracle also helps to address the issue of deliberate

---

[31] Source: https://link.smartcontract.com/whitepaper.

tampering. However, trusted hardware implies trusting the company that produces the hardware, meaning it will always become a centralized point of trust.

Availability—Relying on an oracle service rather than gathering our own data implies that this service should be "always-on" (i.e., available whenever we need it). If we keep using the same oracle service because we trust it, it will be problematic for our company—and our client—if the oracle is not available at a given point in time.

Guaranteeing the availability of oracles is another commitment of Chainlink, as the company seeks to elaborate a validation and reputation system built on their platform oracle list. On the one hand, the validation system offers oracle metrics along with the oracle list. It provides users with an availability rate, as well as a deviation index, which is the percentage of diverging responses from the accepted answer. On the other hand, the reputation system works similarly to those on platforms like TripAdvisor (based on positive or negative reviews). More specifically, the Chainlink reputation system counts the total number of assigned, accepted, and completed requests. It also displays the time to respond and the total penalty received.

To guide clients through the choice of oracles, Chainlink also offers a "certification" system that highlights oracles recognized by the platform as particularly trustworthy and efficient. The company also offers a contract-upgrade service to address dynamic scenarios, which can also be implemented to resolve bugs and remediate hack attempts.

Finally, Chainlink has a native token called Link, which is used to pay oracles for their services; it is also tradeable on exchanges for speculation purposes.

Drawbacks

1) As described, the Chainlink system seems to be quite efficient, but this efficiency comes at a cost. Developers could, for example, skip

the selection service and provide the data by themselves, or they could simply select the cheapest oracle, thus neglecting the most trusted and reliable ones.

2) The Chainlink team takes for granted *the F < N principle*, i.e., that the number of faulty oracles (F) will always be inferior to that of the working oracles (N). This is the same principle of efficiency used in Bitcoin; however, the economic threat posed by the cheater is much stronger than in ChainLink, and the node number is also higher. For this reason, assuming $F < N$, although reasonable, is not always guaranteed.

3) The *deviation index* considers the answer given by an oracle as it compares to the majority. Being deviant, then, is perceived as a negative attribute. However, there is no guarantee that a deviant outcome is a false outcome.

4) The service is decentralized, assuming N (number of working oracles) is large. In statistical research, this is a frequently used assumption that is likely to resolve the problem of biases encountered in a study. However, in reality, N is almost always small; we can assume data is always biased. In the case of Chainlink, then, the platform works for a considerably high number of users, for a considerably large application developer, and for a much larger oracles provider. In turn, the fierce competition between them should make the market righteous and trustworthy. If, on the other hand, in real use cases, the number of developers is low and that of oracles is even lower (which is most likely to happen), the theory may not support the trustworthiness of the network.

5) An intermediary platform should highlight trustworthy providers to its users: it is in the user's best interests to glean more insights on oracles who may/will handle their work more effectively. This type of certification service, however, leads to centralization, which clashes with the guiding principle of decentralization.

Theoretically, only reputations built with time, effort, and cost should be welcomed into the system.

Pythia and Agora

Pythia and Agora[32] are services developed by Delphi Systems to power the Omphalos prediction market. This prediction market embodies a complex system of oracles, tokens, and marketplaces aiming to overcome the oracle problem.

Together, the innovation in Pythia and Agora lies in the addition of a multi-signature component to oracle activity. As with multi-signature wallets, the interaction of more than one entity is required to generate an oracle output. In this specific case, the standard wallet multi-signature system has then been developed to enrich the multi-signature with weight and thresholds.

To better clarify how their design works, I will draw on the innovation example outlined in the company whitepaper.

In this example, we have a total of five oracles. Four of these oracles are assigned a weight of 1, while one is assigned a weight of 3. For the platform to produce an output, a weight of 4 must be reached or surpassed. As shown in the figures below, this is only possible under two conditions:[33]

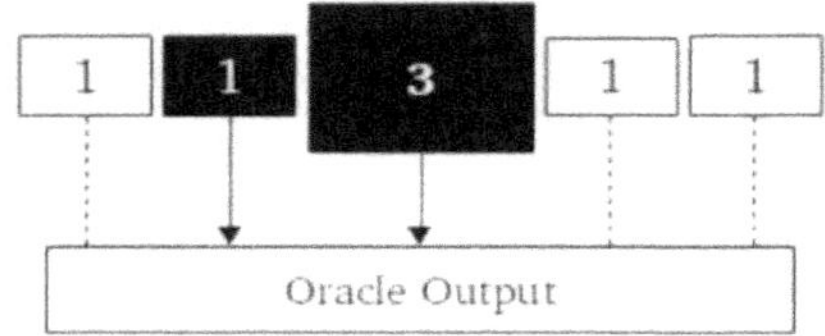

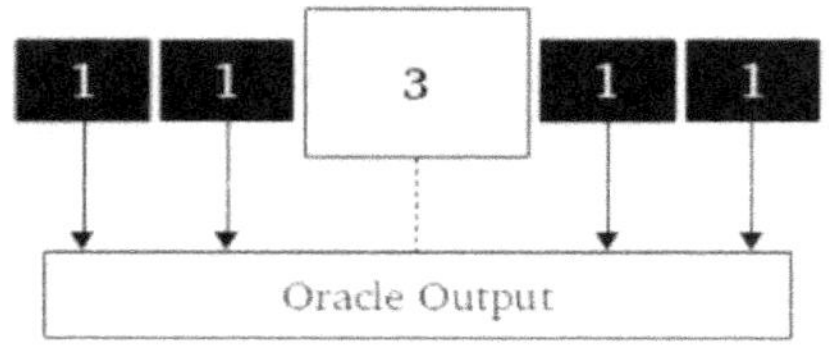

To reach a consensus, either the 3-weighted oracle (or *alpha oracle*) must agree with the 1-weighted oracles (or *subsidiary oracles*), or all four subsidiary oracles must be in agreement. Significantly, even giving a different weight to the oracles does not allow one entity to decide the

---

[32] Source: https://delphi.systems/.
[33] Source: https://delphi.systems/whitepaper.pdf.

output of a contract. If the alpha oracle, for example, displays an outcome that diverges from the four subsidiaries, it will still be unable to affect the contract. In other words, no single party is able to make a decision unilaterally, so the output cannot be considered centralized. There is no other consensus mechanism apart from the weights and the threshold. Once a certain weight is reached, an output is produced.

As the developer states, the weighting of oracles is subject to change depending on their activity. A trustworthy oracle is expected to weigh more, while a faulty oracle should weigh less or be expelled from the system.

As oracles are recognized as selfish entities, their work demands remuneration. Tokens are therefore crucial to the development and functioning of the platform. Delphi Systems have opted for the interaction of more than one token to better handle the platform's different purposes. The minimal token (called PHI) is mostly used for transactions. It is more likely to be used for oracle payments or for speculation purposes as an easy and cheap token to exchange.

Then there is a signal token (sPHI), which is intended more for functionality purposes. The signal token is more versatile and memorizes a snapshot of the balance every time it is transferred. These characteristics make it more suitable for reviews, rating systems, and polling purposes. Being easily traceable, it could also prevent Sybil attacks[34] and provide greater insight into oracles' reputations. However, the higher versatility of the sPHI token corresponds to higher transaction costs, making it less appealing for simple transactions. The platform also offers a dedicated section for exchanging PHI and sPHI tokens, allowing users to benefit from both.

Agora is a decentralized oracle marketplace within the virtual Delphi ecosystem. It is here that oracles are chosen. Users can browse oracle

---

[34] See the appendix section for a detailed explanation of sybil attacks.

characteristics and select the most cost-effective solution for their purposes. Since weight/threshold is the only consensus mechanism present, data analytics play a fundamental role in the platform's successful management. On the other hand, data analytics can be easily done due to the snapshot mechanism introduced with the sPHI token.

The developer has stated that, although the system was built on Ethereum, it is also intended to be operative on Bitcoin as well as other platforms. Although first deployed in their prediction market, the oracle marketplace may therefore be used for other purposes and compete with other platforms such as Augur.

Drawbacks

1) The multi-signature system is exciting but shallow. Aside from the authors' basic examples, the whitepaper lacks a more concrete example of contracts to clearly show the system's advantages in real use cases.
2) If weight and threshold are said to be variable, this means that an initial value has to be assigned to each oracle. It is not clear, however, how this initial value is assigned and how it is changed over time. Does the developer have any influence on the value allocation?
3) This project appears to be developed as an Augur competitor, with only minimal changes. At present, it is unclear why it would be more convenient to use this system than the more well-known Augur platform.
4) The rewards system for oracles and the oracle selection and punishment criteria seem to lack clear working definitions.

Provable (Oraclize)

Provable[35] (previously known as Oraclize) claims to be the leading oracle service for smart contracts and blockchain applications. Their service is available on platforms like Ethereum, Rootstock, R3 Corda, Hyperledger Fabric, and EOS.

Provable's solution to the oracle problem differs slightly from other proposals. The common approach, as we have seen, is to propose a decentralized system of oracles or marketplaces. Provable, on the other hand, seeks to produce trusted output through a consensus mechanism based on reputation or thresholds, even drawing data from untrusted sources.

Provable aims to demonstrate that the data fetched by the oracle is genuine and untampered. The company claims to accomplish this by presenting the returned data along with a document called an "authenticity proof."

These authenticity proofs can be built using different technologies, such as auditable virtual machines and Trusted Execution Environments. This resolves the oracle problem by transferring trust away from Provable and into the certification. The solution is also highly interoperable since data providers do not have to modify their services to be compatible with blockchain protocols. Smart contracts can, therefore, directly access data from websites or APIs. The platform has also been built to be easily integrated with both private and public instances of various blockchain protocols.

The Provable engine is structured in a relatively elementary way. Recalling the flow function (if -> then), it executes a request once specific conditions are met. A valid data request to the engine should indicate the query, the data source type, and (where possible) the type of certification required.

---

[35] Source: https://provable.xyz/.

The query is like a question that we wish to answer thanks to the oracle. It is written in programming language and appears as follows:[36]

provable_query("URL", "json(https://shapeshift.io/sendamount).success.deposit",

'{"pair":"eth_btc","amount":"1","withdrawal":"1AAcCo21EUc1jbocjssSQDzLna9Vem2UN5"
}')

Although in the future it may be possible to write queries as discursive questions, at present, a decent working knowledge of programming languages is required to write queries. Data source type, on the other hand, can most likely be anything digital. The Provable engine supports URLs, scripts, the output of computations, and so on.

As for the certification requested, the developer specifies that a limited set of certifications is available according to the chosen data source. Proofs are then verifiable using dedicated verification tools.

While the Provable system is rather simple in its concept, the developers also provide an in-depth guide and tutorial on how to implement it with various blockchain platforms.

Drawbacks

1) In essence, Provable solves the oracle problem by applying centralization to a decentralized application. Although it may work, it nevertheless represents a controversial and debatable approach.
2) The service provides external data for smart contracts when the developer has no other means to gather it. It is not an alternative but a solution when there are no other choices.
3) Trusting Provable is therefore a must when using their system (*"Oraclize is not trustless but provably honest"*).

---

[36] Source: https://docs.provable.xyz/.

4) Transport Layer Security (TLS) notary proofs aim to show that Provable has not altered the fetched data, but this does not prove that the source data is reliable.

5) In principle, Provable has no technical vulnerabilities or weaknesses. However, it will share the same vulnerabilities and weaknesses of the platform on which it operates. For example, if operating on Ethereum, it will suffer from high costs, absence of confidentiality/privacy, and low scalability. Queries, however, can still be encrypted for privacy purposes.

Closing remarks

In this chapter, we looked at some of the proposed ways to address the oracle problem. All of them are interesting and powerful. But none is 100% effective.

Another possibility is that none of these systems will prevail and that they will all coexist. According to the specific sector or industry, one particular approach may prove more effective than the others. In the next chapter, we will turn to real-world applications in industries.

Takeaway: An important threat to decentralized oracle applications is the so-called *Sybil attack*. You can find more details about this kind of attack in the appendix of this book.

Chapter 6

The oracle problem in real-world blockchains

Having explored the concepts of blockchain, smart contracts, oracles, and the oracle problem, we can now turn to how the oracle problem can interfere with the development of real-world applications—in supply chains, healthcare, intellectual property, and so on.

Recently, researchers and enthusiasts have proposed blockchain applications for all sorts of companies and industries. However, every real-world application comes up against the oracle problem, although the impacts and consequences may differ. This chapter analyzes some of these applications to understand how the blockchain oracle problem may affect their future development.

Intellectual property rights protection

Among academics and professionals, opinion suggests that the original purpose of the blockchain—before the crypto era—was to "register" intellectual property rights (IPRs).

In the early 1990s, two cryptographers, Stuart Haber and W. Scott Stornetta, published an article in the *Journal of Cryptology* in which they proposed the digital timestamping of documents in sequence to authenticate authorship of intellectual property. Satoshi Nakamoto then referred to this type of structure as a "chain of blocks," which we now call blockchain.

Due to the incredible rise in the price of Bitcoin, the financial applications of blockchain overshadowed the role it plays in the protection of IPRs. However, this role aroused interest again after smart contract platforms like EVMs became functional and well-known.

Changes or advancements in the IPR field have been sought to affect many industries, but the music industry is thought to be the most impacted by blockchains in response to unfair record label practices[37], as well as the digital revolution. The changes promoted by blockchain adoption in the industry grant artists the ability to determine prices for their songs independently and to autonomously license their works. This *direct-to-fan* trend enables the artist to customize their offer completely. Examples and pilot projects include Mycelia, Monegraf, PoE, and UJO. According to the programmed smart contracts, royalties are also distributed more fairly and efficiently. However, experts in the field have raised concerns over the *attestation service* on the blockchain platform, which is actually a form of oracle.

If the system works correctly, data is protected against tampering when successfully uploaded to the blockchain. Furthermore, if the smart contracts are bug-free, they will efficiently share revenues among authors. The weak point of the system, however, remains the gateway between the author and the blockchain. While anyone who uploads a piece of art is recognized as the "owner" of the digital record, the system is unable to verify if it has been stolen or just given by someone else.

In response to this issue, *proof of authority* (PoA) provides artists with timestamped evidence of digital creation. This timestamp is vital since it can be used in the case of IPR claims.

However, as the timestamp can only provide the upload's exact time, it cannot verify the original production's real authorship. In the case of artists noticing their own work being registered by someone else, there will always be the need for a legal system to enforce the IPRs and react to violations. In the absence of such an authority, the blockchain may end up

---

[37] Hughes et al. (2019) : Beyond Bitcoin: What blockchain and distributed ledger technologies mean for firms. Business Horizons. Vol. 62, pp. 273-281

being a first-come-first-serve platform, where the only thing that counts is to be the first to upload the artwork.

The critical consensus would suggest that it is unlikely that the system could be wholly automatized and self-sufficient. However, decentralization of the service may reduce centralized authorities' power and help artists have greater control over their creations.

Now, since the action of uploading the art is so determinant, it is hard to tell if this must be done by the author or by an external authority that ensures the authenticity and authorship of a creation. In this context, the oracle problem means deciding whether the author or a legal authority should fulfill the role of the oracle. From a technical point of view, they are both equally capable and entitled to serve as oracles, but the decision is significant from a social point of view.

If the authors themselves play the role of oracle, companies like the record labels will lose their power in favor of artists. If artists can obtain the copyright by uploading their content directly on the blockchain, they will no longer be kept in check by the record labels. Furthermore, the smart contract can also decide the distribution of royalties for the sales of their creations as well as the blockchain fees.[38]

On the other hand, if the power to upload the authorship data is given to the record label, then the situation will pretty much remain as it is. The certification system will simply switch from a legacy database to a blockchain equivalent without any disruptive changes. In this case, the need for a blockchain becomes questionable.

A third scenario would see external parties—neither authors nor labels—in charge of uploading documents and setting up smart contracts on behalf

---

[38] For smart contract applications, fees are made up of two components. Just like normal transactions, one part of the fees is sent to the miners. However, another part can be taken by the contract creator to run the service. Such costs can make smart contract applications extremely costly to execute.

of the authors. This option would reduce the risk of errors or faulty contracts, but third-party dependency still represents a problem.

In reality, it is clear that the legal aspect of protecting intellectual property is unlikely to be separated from central authorities. Applying a blockchain that relies on third parties will not eliminate intermediaries but simply create new ones.

The following figure summarizes the dilemma of the *twin* oracle problem:

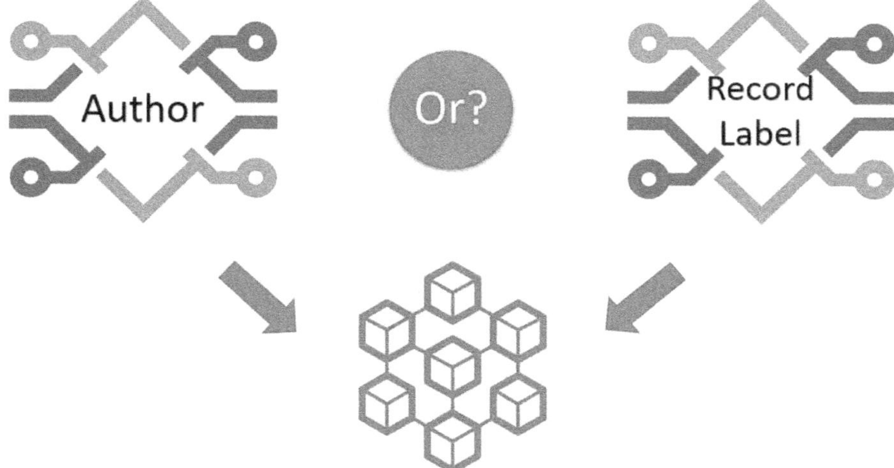

Academic transcripts

Another objective of decentralized technologies is systemic improvement in the field of education. As researchers have reaffirmed, blockchain applications seek to solve privacy, security, and vulnerability issues in the *"ubiquitous learning environment."*[39]

---

[39] Bdiwi et al. (2017): Towards a New Ubiquitous Learning Environment Based on blockchain technology. IEEE ICALT 2017, Timisoara, Romania, 3–7 July 2017; pp. 101–102.

More specifically, blockchain applications could enhance the digital accreditation of personal and academic learning, improving complex credit management, such as the European Credit Transfer Accumulation System (ECTS). At present, the most advanced institutions in the field are as follows:

1) The University Media Lab at the Massachusetts Institute of Technology (MIT) has developed Blockcert, a software that works on top of a blockchain. As it is *blockchain-agnostic*, it can be adapted to different platforms and implemented on Bitcoin, Ethereum, or IBM's Hyperledger Fabric.

2) The University of Nicosia (UNIC), part of the Blockcert consortium, has developed a software named Block.co. The innovative aspect of this software is that it permits the upload of certificates in bulk, with a consistent reduction in time and costs.

3) Sony Corporation has developed Sony Global Education (SGE) in cooperation with Hyperledger Fabric. The aim of SGE is to empower the connection between humans and machines, offering specialized courses focused on tasks that only humans can perform.

Despite the low speed of the Bitcoin blockchain (due to the block time set at 10 minutes) and the high costs of its cryptocurrency, the most advanced institutions in the education field have tended to prefer the Bitcoin network to register their academic transcripts. This is likely because Bitcoin has such a large network and a stable user base; it is also associated with robust financial investment and thus is considered to have a better chance of survival.

From a user perspective, I can say that it is very straightforward to interact with blockchain-based academic transcripts. My first direct experience was with UNIC, which launched a MOOC on Blockchain and Digital Currencies in 2014.

Upon completion of the course, UNIC issues a certificate like the one below:

The certificate received is analogous in its structure to those issued by other universities worldwide. It is also sent as a PDF attachment, meaning no specialized hardware or software is required to open it.

Crucially, the advantage of blockchain certification lies in its ability to determine its authenticity quickly and effortlessly. Understanding whether a certificate is genuine or not does not require any specialized examination or intervention from the issuing institution.

In the case of the University of Nicosia, there is a dedicated section on their website to verify the authenticity of certificates from their institutions:[40]

---

[40] Source: www.unic.ac.cy/verify/.

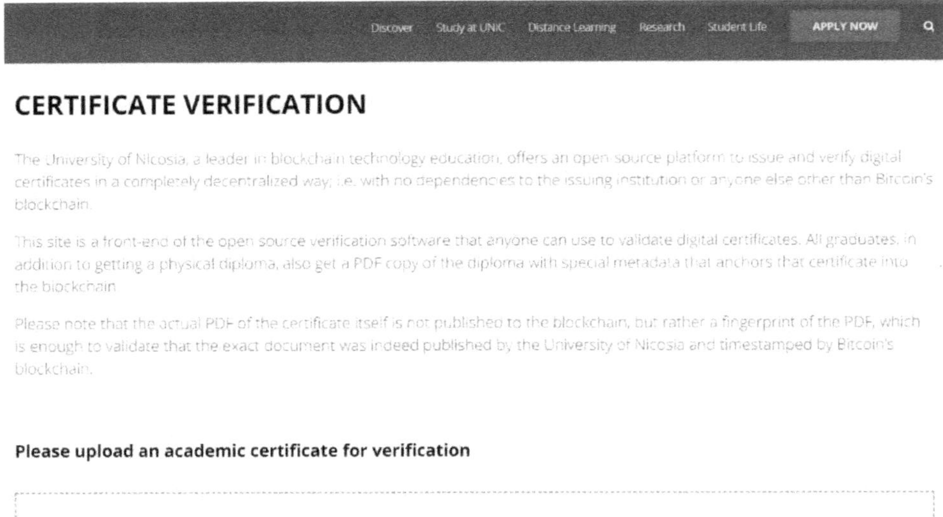

To authenticate a transcript, the user simply needs to follow the on-page instructions and drop the PDF into the dedicated space.

For my own certification, for example, we obtain the following result:

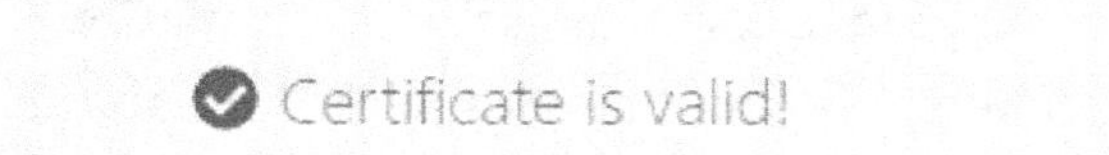

✅ Certificate is valid!

Issuer ❓

University of Nicosia

Issuer verification ❓
Block.co verified the identity of this issuer ✅ ❓

Blockchain ❓
Bitcoin

Issuer ID ❓
1A94iDxxJijPvo8CjCWe4GLUfT6BGTWuUq

Issuance transaction ID ❓
16345cd64c69aff923c700202c26ae67618d26a438183a57a9539e76b2b5c9d1

Block timestamp ❓
📅 2019-12-18   🕐 16:26

Additional Information	
First name	Giulio
Last name	Caldarelli
Grade %	90.33
Date	17/12/2019

Now, let us hypothesize that someone wants to alter the certificate. Due to the intrinsic economic value of academic certification, this is already a common issue for institutions: recent research has shown that an increasing number of fake certificates are in circulation.[41] And it is not only desperate jobseekers who are using fake credentials; students, managers, even politicians have been found to try their luck with them.

These days, with practically any PC, it is possible to forge academic certificates with minimal effort. So, to verify if the system really worked, I altered my own certificate and reuploaded it to see if the forgery was detected. (Try to spot the tampered section!)

Tampered certificate

Reuploading the certificate to the same website section resulted in the following warning message:

---

[41] Untung Rahardja et al., "Authenticity of a Diploma Using the Blockchain Approach." *International Journal of Advanced Trends in Computer Science and Engineering* 9, no. 1.2 (2020): 250–256.

In case you didn't notice, I altered the certificate's issue date from 2019 to 2017, but the same warning would have been triggered for any modified content. Indeed, simply adding or removing a dot in the text would have led to the same outcome.

This is undoubtedly a powerful system, but as with other real-world applications, academic ones are not exempt from the oracle problem.

As universities are themselves oracles, their blockchain data is as trustworthy as the institution itself. Arguably, what makes information on the blockchain more reliable is the level of trust that we place directly in the oracle (institution). But trust can never be considered as a binary, or what we call a *dummy* variable in research.[42]

Trust is never completely absent or present in a relationship; it is measured by degree. We can trust two people, but not to the same extent. We may trust our neighbors to water our plants when we are out of town, but would we also entrust our children to them? In turn, can we assume that, since academic institutions are trusted entities, their uploaded data should also be "fully trusted"?

---

[42] A variable is called dummy or binary if it can take only two values (e.g., 0/1, male/female).

If the data is directly uploaded by the certifying institutions, we are unable to verify its integrity; there is no way to provide this data *trustlessly*. As oracles, the universities are providing their own subjective truth, and we must accept it at face value.

The oracle problem for academic institutions, then, revolves around the degree of trust that we assign to each institution. Granted, most universities have a long-standing reputation, which makes their information more or less reliable depending on their history. In general, if a certificate is on a blockchain, its authenticity can indeed be proven. But what cannot be verified is the truthfulness of the data that the certificate reports.

For example, if students obtain their degree from a low-ranked university, the fact that their certificates are on the blockchain does not give a higher value to the record. If a degree has been bought, the document will still show as "authentic" on the blockchain. Ultimately, the extrinsic value of an academic document is always given only and exclusively by the reputation of the institution issuing the certificate.

For applications in which a single institution or entity fulfills the oracle role, the trust cannot be shifted from the institution to the system:

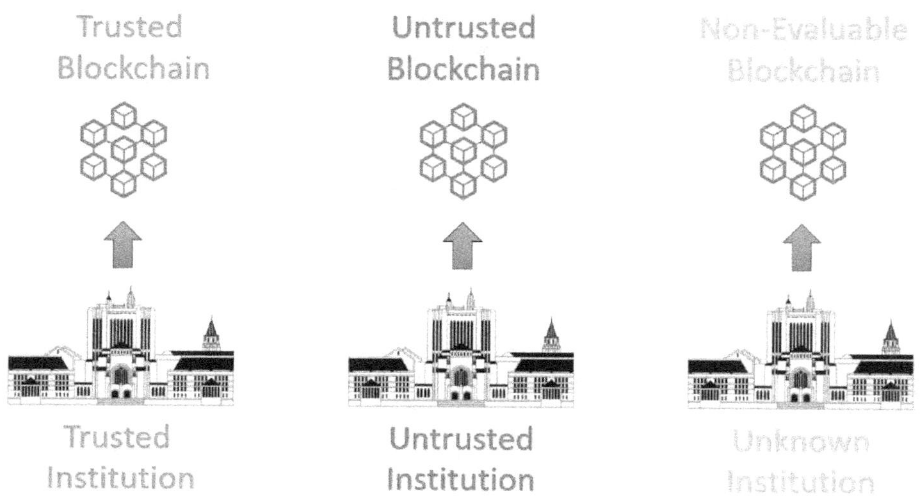

Supply chain and traceability

Many researchers have investigated and supported blockchain applications for secure data provenance.

Blockchain allows the user to trace the origin of a Bitcoin safely, quickly, and trustlessly. Experts then hypothesized that blockchain would enable the tracing of real-world assets with the same degree of reliability. The security and immutability features of blockchains would help to ensure provenance and safety for shipments of drugs, food, and other critical assets.

However, in his provocatively-titled "Bananas on the Blockchain" speech, Andreas Antonopoulos brilliantly explained why and how linking a real product to the blockchain should raise concerns about the reliability of this traceability system.

When dealing with cryptocurrencies, the provenance of a Bitcoin is guaranteed since it was 'born' on the blockchain, and every movement from first issuance can be tracked in the immutable and transparent ledger. On the contrary, for a real-world product like a mango sitting on a supermarket shelf, the provenance is unknown to the blockchain, and oracles must insert the necessary origin data.

In supply chain applications, oracles typically belong to (or are strictly controlled by) the company producing the tracked goods. As you can imagine, this represents a significant conflict of interest. While blockchain/oracle services may be outsourced to a third party (e.g., Chainlink, Provable), the control over information remains in the supplier's hands. The supplier therefore decides what information to upload to the blockchain, and it is unlikely to spot erroneous or unwanted data.

From this, we can surmise that, for real-world goods (tangible or intangible), data on the blockchain is immutable but not unquestionable and that information is only as reliable as the company that owns the supply chain.

A recent academic study has also discussed the reliability of supply in private and consortium blockchains, raising the same doubts over the oracle problem.[43] Such problems arise in all blockchain types since the oracle problem is both technical and social. Assuming that both private and public blockchains work perfectly, the trustworthiness of the processed data has nothing to do with their technical functioning.

Another project in my own department considered the oracle problem in the traceability of dairy products. We looked at an Italian producer of a high-quality cheese that is subject to strict procedural guidelines to obtain a mark of provenance called DOP ("Denominazione di Origine Protetta," literally "Designation of Protected Origin"). The certification authority ensures that the company follows the rules prescribed in the guidelines and can issue fines for non-compliance. Due to a rise in product counterfeiting, the company decided to trace its product on the blockchain, ensuring that clients could identify the genuine cheese and avoid buying counterfeit versions.

The company developed the traceability of their goods using the Ethereum blockchain. Data is uploaded to the blockchain through a service company, which also fulfills the role of oracle. As a result, it is the most likely to upload untrusted data to the blockchain.

However, since the product is subject to strict DOP regulations, uploaded data cannot diverge from what the supervising authority inspects. Deciding to upload deviant data to the blockchain would be detrimental, as it would then be impossible for the company to delete the false data. With this mechanism of incentives and deterrents, also known as *the trust*

---

[43] Akhil Kumar, Rong Liu, and Zhe Shan, "Is Blockchain a Silver Bullet for Supply Chain Management? Technical Challenges and Research Opportunities," *Decision Sciences* 51, no. 1 (2020): 8–37.

model, we believe that data uploaded on the blockchain is more trustworthy than when no third-party supervising authority is involved.

It would appear, then, that the oracle problem for the traceability of products can be partially overcome by creating the right trust model. In our cheesemaking example, trust is shifted not to the system or to the producer but to the supervising authority:

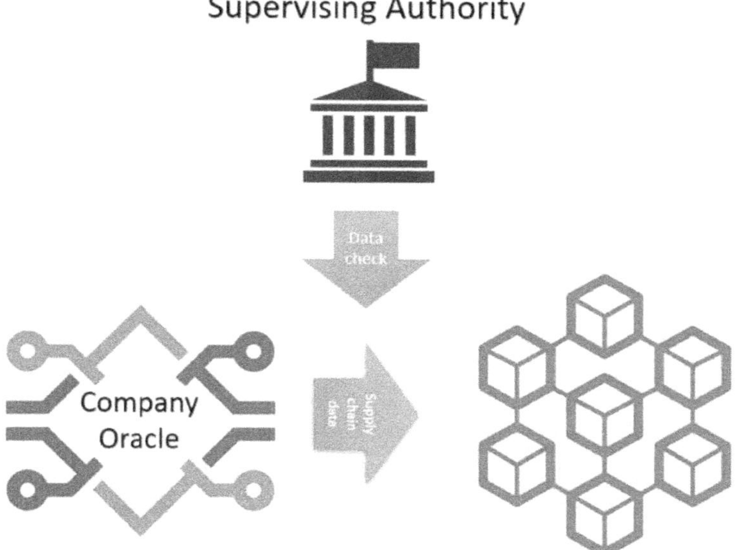

With a well-built and detailed trust model, the likelihood that information on the blockchain could diverge from reality will be low. However, if the market is local, the product is fungible, and the production is not supervised by any third-party authority, designing a trust model will be much more difficult. Furthermore, the need for a blockchain would also be questionable.

Energy

The most cited advantages of introducing blockchains in the energy sector are marketplace cost reduction and increased transparency and decentralization.

Although I cannot recall many active projects, the Energy Internet and the Brooklyn microgrid have undoubtedly raised expectations in the field.

Unfortunately, the finer details of how blockchains could help improve the energy sector are often neglected or even unmentioned in proposals. I have recently published a couple of academic articles discussing the fact that, to date, no contribution has yet addressed the oracle problem in the energy field. This is critical and troubling, since the oracle problem in the energy field is highly problematic.

In resource management, whether it is water, oil, gas, or electricity, the oracle problem is a "dual" one, since it affects both inbound and outbound transactions. If the platform is blockchain-based, we will have an inbound transaction when resources are transferred to the platform and then an outbound transaction when resources are requested elsewhere. In both cases, the intervention of oracles is required to ensure that the resources are transferred correctly. And the inbound and outbound oracles will most likely be different devices or entities.

To better understand how complicated this system is, we can consider the example of a prosumer. As shown in the figure below, a prosumer is someone who acquires energy from a centralized provider but who is also capable of producing his own (e.g., using solar panels). If the prosumer produces more energy than what he consumes, he can sell the excess on an energy marketplace.

Let's assume that this marketplace operates on a blockchain. To allow data about the prosumer's contribution to be uploaded to the blockchain, we need at least one inbound oracle (sensor) to collect data from his household. Regardless of whether the oracle is owned by the prosumer or the platform, its position will be known. But having the oracle in his proximity or control gives the prosumer the highest incentive to manipulate the sensor to send false data about his contribution. To anticipate this, the platform should deploy a second oracle that double-checks the prosumer's data or use a maintenance service that periodically checks the status of the sensor.

For the reasons outlined above, while the blockchain platform could be decentralized and run independently of a central authority (since nodes may be spread globally, and their exact position is uncertain), oracles are unlikely to be decentralized and autonomous. Sensors (oracles) will more likely be limited in number, placed where the reported event occurs, and linked in some way to a central authority, such as the energy provider or the relevant government agency.

However, this only constitutes half of the problem: the other, more insidious half is the outbound oracle problem.

Considering the same prosumer example, we may also hypothesize that he would like to buy some energy from the blockchain platform during a period when his own production is insufficient. Let's assume that the blockchain will promptly execute the transaction correctly, transferring the prosumer's funds to the platform account. The blockchain should then communicate with an external system to ensure that the exact amount of energy is sent to the prosumer.

However, from that point, countless events may alter the real-world procedure. We may encounter a bug in the smart contract, sensor malfunction, scarcity of resources, failure of the power plants, cable sabotage, or authority denial. Also, the non-existence of the physical structure may not prevent the smart contract from being successfully executed.

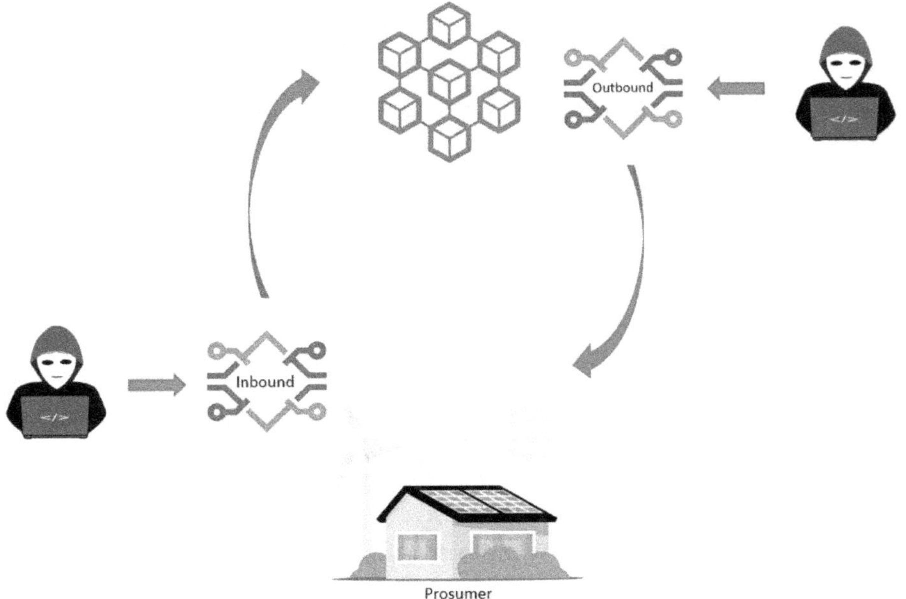

As a result, an external authority that monitors these procedures is essential for the system to work correctly and to ensure that the prosumer is refunded in the case of malfunction. Again, it is improbable that this external authority or organization will be free or independent from the energy supplier or government.

Other hypothetical blockchain applications abound in the resource management sector, but they all share the same inbound/outbound oracle problem. Unfortunately, to date, empirical research is still lacking into how the "dual" oracle problem can be addressed.

Contracting and law

According to Andrès Guadamuz, the state of Arizona has made the first attempt to regulate smart contracts. There, state law defines smart contracts as *"event-driven programs, with a state that runs on a distributed, decentralized, shared, and replicated ledger, and that can take custody over and instruct transfer of assets on that ledger."* Stating that smart contracts run on 'something,' however, obligates legislators to define the platform on which they operate. Unfortunately, we still have no unique definition of blockchain; indeed, the Arizona legislators encountered a problem in elaborating the text, defining blockchain as a *"distributed ledger technology that uses a distributed, decentralized, shared, and replicated ledger, which may be public or private, permissioned, or permissionless, or driven by tokenized crypto-economic or token-less. The data on the ledger is protected with cryptography, is immutable and auditable, and provides an uncensored truth."*

This definition is overly general and bears a number of important contradictions. If it is private, a blockchain is neither an open ledger nor a distributed one. Furthermore, the concept of "uncensored truth" is rather controversial. If the system runs well, we may achieve immutability, but the veracity of the ledger's information can hardly be proven as a result of the oracle problem.

Legal researchers were among the first to recognize that the problem with a smart contract involving real-world data arises from the presence of third parties (oracles) external to the contractors whose legal state is yet to be identified. When signing or executing smart contracts, parties cannot fully trust each other, and an oracle is in the best position to manipulate the data and collude with one of the parties.

In a recent academic study, Matija Damjan[44] has noted that services offering oracles (e.g., Provable, Reality Keys) do not guarantee oracle impartiality or the veracity of the information provided. They therefore negate the two necessary conditions for smart contracts to be implemented for legal purposes.

---

[44] Damjan M. (2018): The interface between blockchain and the real world. Ragion Pratica

In another legal essay, Jens Frankenreiter[45] has identified four critical issues related to smart contracts and oracles, even hypothesizing their good faith.

First, as an oracle is to be trusted, its identity must be known, which poses a threat to its impartiality and independence. While governments cannot change information on the blockchain, they can influence oracles by exerting pressure on the organization controlling them.

Second, linking certain real-world assets (cheese, car, stocks, land titles) to a blockchain token cannot be done without the intervention of legal authorities. If the blockchain platform is decentralized and autonomous, the system will only display that a transaction has been executed. However, what happens in the real world cannot be influenced without the presence of an authority to enforce the contracts.

Third, since oracles can be sensors or humans, they are not 100% reliable, even if they are trustworthy. If a malfunction occurs (or if the contract is not executed correctly), the platform cannot restore the original state or provide compensation for a breakdown. The presence of an external authority (capable of enforcing a malfunctioning smart contract) is hence necessary for all parties to completely trust the system.

There is also a fourth point to consider. Decentralized platforms on which smart contracts run and operate are dependent on the efforts of miners, who are not platform employees; their contribution is based on the expected rewards. When Bitcoin first launched, perhaps the miners contributed for fun or because they believed in the system, but now they are mostly represented by companies that have invested millions of dollars in mining technologies and are expecting sizable returns. This means that, as long as the market and the price of currencies make it sustainable, the miners will keep contributing to the security of the system. If mining is no longer worth the effort, the miners will leave the system, eventually

---

[45] Frankenreiter J. (2019) : The limits of smart contracts. J. Inst. Theor. Econ.

decreasing the platform's security level. If the legal system is based on a blockchain, such a shock to the market could jeopardize the reliability of the entire system.

From a legal point of view, it is also interesting to understand the implications of illegal contracts or activities performed on a blockchain. As decentralized autonomous organizations, blockchains are not subject to any law. However, as oracles are neither independent nor decentralized, they could constitute an effective means of regulating blockchain-based organizations.

Healthcare

Many possible implementations of blockchains in the healthcare sector have been forwarded by practitioners and academics alike. Practical experiments and pilot projects have highlighted potential blockchain integration in health records, health insurance, biomedical research, drug supply, and medical education.

Despite the variety of the proposals, above all, applying blockchain in healthcare aims to improve data privacy and security. This choice is justified given that privacy and security breaches are increasing exponentially every year. Cybersecurity research, for example, has revealed that 37 million medical records were illegally accessed between 2010 and 2017, with 300[46] breaches alone in 2017.[47] Furthermore, there is still no unified system to store and distribute patient information between healthcare facilities.

Countless proposals and concepts of blockchain applications have been discussed to overcome these issues. Here are some of the best known and successful projects:

---

[46] Every breach involves hundreds or thousands of patients' records.

[47] Thomas H. McCoy and Roy H. Perlis, "Temporal Trends and Characteristics of Reportable Health Data Breaches, 2010–2017," *Journal of the American Medical Association* 320, no. 12 (2018): 1282–84.

Dentacoin (www.dentacoin.com) works very similarly to platforms such as TripAdvisor; through a stringent reviews system, it ensures that doctors are appropriately qualified to operate in the dental industry.

Solve.Care (www.solve.care) provides a platform that manages access to care and payments, making healthcare more affordable and user-friendly.

Medibloc (www.medibloc.org) provides a private and reliable blockchain to store and distribute medical data.

Medicalchain (www.medicalchain.com) offers a solution for personal health records storage, also providing a direct link with insurance companies.

Lockpharma (www.lockpharma.pl) ensures the traceability and authenticity of drugs using blockchain and the Internet of Things (quick response code).

Blockchain applications are implemented to meet different healthcare needs, and the oracle structure differs according to the offered service. Yet the oracle problem is particularly controversial in this sector.

For example, applications like Dentacoin are analogous to the Augur prediction market (see Chapter 4). Since the oracles are the same people uploading reviews, their trustworthiness relies on the wisdom of the crowd and therefore shares the same strengths and weaknesses. Lockpharma, on the other hand, as a means to track medical goods, responds to the same rules discussed in the supply chain section above: oracles require an external authority to confirm the data they upload about the traceability of products. Furthermore, the QR code as an image can be easily altered if sophisticated countermeasures (such as holograms) are not implemented.

In attempts to offer a unified platform where patient data can be universally accessible yet secure and private, the common structure is a permissioned blockchain in which certain users have the "rights" to upload healthcare data to the platform. In this structure, a central platform operates on a blockchain, while a distributed system of oracles uploads the patient data.

Discussing the oracle problem in such cases is incredibly complex.

First, it must be decided whether the patient or the healthcare institution should have the right to upload the data to the blockchain. This dilemma echoes that of the intellectual property cases outlined earlier in this chapter. If it is the patient who decides, the health institution could ensure that the data is inserted correctly and that no erroneous information has been uploaded. Otherwise, both patient and institution could be blockchain oracles and "granted" the right to upload different pieces of data.

However, in a system like this, the more oracles we have, the greater the chances that data may be tampered with or incorrect. Equally, having more oracles does not imply that they are distributed. If every oracle is in charge of uploading a different piece of data, the effect is the same as with centralization. Uncertainty around data provenance could also affect system reliability since we will never know which (or how many) data sources are trustworthy.

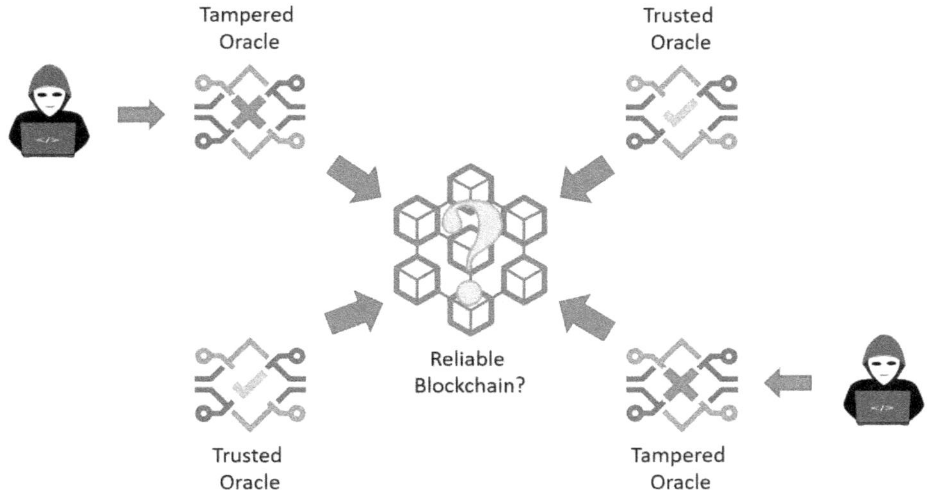

In the end, though, I share the thinking of those academics who believe that the risk of data imprecision is outweighed by the potential benefits of having a global healthcare record, which could prove lifesaving in an emergency or pandemic. Interestingly, Solve.Care has recently signed an agreement with Chainlink to use external oracles to supervise the insertion of sensitive data on the blockchain. Although promising, the reliability of this project has yet to be verified.

Open challenges

In a recent research paper, I produced a table illustrating the different impacts of the oracle problem depending on the sector involved. The idea was to draw from each sector the implications that represented a challenge to blockchain reliability, which could then be further analyzed and more effectively addressed.

Condition	Description	Implication	Example
Trusted Oracle Problem	Extent to which a specific oracle is perceived as trustworthy	Untrusted oracle leads to untrusted blockchain data	Academic records, Supply chain
Dual Oracle Problem	Condition in which oracles intervene in two (or more) different and unrelated stages of blockchain application	Tampering or malfunction by one oracle undermines the whole process	Resource management (e.g., energy)
Multiple Oracle Problem	Data are verified and uploaded on the blockchain by multiple oracles	Practical for publicly available data; proven to be a point of failure for sensitive and private data	Health records, Entertainment
Hierarch Oracle Problem	Certain oracles have predominance over others	Smart contracts may be denied or reverted	Contracting, Law
Twin Oracle Problem	Oracles are equally valid but are substitutes	The choice of oracle gives greater power to one party over the other	IPRs protection

Trusted oracle problem

The trusted oracle problem is a highly controversial condition, in which we have a single source of data whose veracity cannot be verified by external parties. Academic transcripts are a perfect example, as are local supply chains. When data has to be uploaded on the blockchain, the data source is directly owned and controlled by institutions or companies, and there is apparently no means to verify if those actors are uploading accurate and reliable data. This is exclusively a trust problem since, if you trust the institution/company, you trust the oracle and the data on the blockchain. If you do not, then the blockchain implementation does not matter at all.

Dual oracle problem

The dual oracle problem refers to the condition in which blockchain applications involve both an inbound and outbound flow of data, as with resource management, for instance. The problem here is based on the unlikelihood that two connected oracle systems can work without support from a third party that monitors the correct execution of operations. Since it is already difficult for a single oracle system to work without malfunction or tampering, the possibility that two connected oracle systems can operate without issue or supervision is extremely remote. Furthermore, the possibility of having a working system of outbound oracles is still widely debated.

Multiple oracle problem

The multiple oracle problem is apparent in applications that naturally involve more than one oracle. Whereas multiple oracles may bring more reliability to the data provided in gaming or financial services, for example, for applications such as healthcare, the same condition may prove controversial. If multiple oracles upload data to the blockchain, we will have the coexistence of data with varying levels of reliability/trustworthiness. As a result, the whole system's reliability will be unknown.

Hierarch oracle problem

At the time of writing, the hierarch oracle problem is a condition that does not exist yet. Rather, it is a conjecture based largely on the work of legal researchers. Since the legal system is itself based on disputes, the indisputability of smart contracts is not perceived as an ideal solution. Indeed, there is the real problem of guaranteeing that the outcomes of smart contracts do not harm anyone. For these reasons, proposals have argued for the introduction of oracles whose roles and functions predominate over others. In these cases, we may have independent oracles (*slaves*) controlled by other oracles (*hierarchs*) managed by governments. While I am not in the position to discuss the merit of such proposals, a system like this would undoubtedly require a complex structure of rules, which are yet to be defined.

Twin oracle problem

The twin oracle problem arises in a condition where the technical output is the same regardless of the chosen oracle. The field of intellectual property is the most obvious example. Whether the creator or the authority uploads the data about creation ownership, the information would be the same. But if a contract's outcome is the same, how can we choose the right oracle to upload the data? As explained earlier in the context of the music industry, the chosen oracle will have a predominant role over other parties, and the social outcome of the choice cannot be neglected. However, is it really possible to separate the parties? Should they both constitute an oracle? Unfortunately, we still have no answers to these questions.

Conclusions

The aim of this book was to give a broad understanding of the concept of oracles and the oracle problem. Chapter 1 outlined the main characteristics of a blockchain and how it works, with a particular focus on the Bitcoin cryptocurrency. Chapter 2 described the smart contract concept and why a new blockchain named Ethereum was necessary. Chapters 3 and 4 focused on oracles, discussing the consequences of their introduction on the reliability of blockchain networks. Chapter 5 illustrated some active projects and proposals that provide oracle services with the intent of overcoming the oracle problem, discussing their respective strengths and weaknesses. Chapter 6 projected the oracle problem onto real-world blockchain applications and outlined oracle implementation issues in various industries, along with open challenges.

Presenting and reflecting on the limitations of oracles is by no means intended as a critique of the technology. I believe that a broader understanding of the real potential of blockchains is especially useful for entrepreneurs who can benefit from this powerful technology. Books have the power to reach people from different backgrounds; given the complexity of the challenges presented herein, a wider audience is needed to overcome them. I hope that this book raises some awareness and draws attention to the phenomenon so that more people can investigate the oracle problem and its potential resolutions. In the future, I will also endeavor to update the present work with the latest research, discoveries, and (hopefully) useful solutions.

Again, thank you very much for reading my book!

Appendix

This section outlines certain concepts that I believe are essential to the complete understanding of the book's content. For organizational and logical reasons, these were not inserted into the main body text. In future editions, I may also reorganize chapters to include them or further enrich this section with other key concepts.

Oracles on the Bitcoin blockchain

As stated in Chapter 2, smart contracts cannot be stored directly on the Bitcoin blockchain. Unlike with Ethereum, there is no way to store the code and select an on-chain oracle to collect data from the external world. Some services will let you store and operate contracts on external layers, but this means losing out on the benefits associated with decentralization. With bitcoin scripts, you can operate directly on the Bitcoin blockchain, but you should always rely on oracles to fetch real-world data.

Now, since oracles are queried thanks to smart contracts, a workaround was needed to operate them on Bitcoin. This was achieved by exploiting multi-signature transactions. As explained in Chapter 1, M-of-N multi-signature transactions require more than one signature to perform a transaction. While one signature is usually inserted when the script is generated, the second is added when a certain condition is verified.

Let's look at the example of the timelock bitcoin script. As we know, timelock scripts ensure that a certain transaction happens at a precise moment or after a predetermined amount of time. In this case, while one signature is added at script creation, the second is added when the required amount of time has elapsed. Basically, the oracle is the owner of the second key and fulfills the role of making sure that his key signs the transaction at the right time.

This workaround is effective and typically does not require any additional feature to be performed. However, within these scripts, the oracle problem lies in the second key owner's reliability, which must be trusted. And if smart contracts involving Bitcoin blockchains are executed elsewhere (with the aid of external layers or protocols), then all platforms and oracles should be trusted too.

The Sybil attack

In principle, the Sybil attack is not necessarily related to computer science: it is used as a catch-all term for an attempt at manipulating democratic choices.

In a democracy, we know that the majority of votes determine the alternative to be followed when it comes to decision-making. There may be various democratic mechanisms (based on thresholds or proportions), but the underlying idea stays the same. Democratic power lies in the fact that different individuals can express their own personal will through their choices. If the majority of people share the same wish, the wish becomes a reality. In essence, it is a means to ensure that what happens is what people really want. Crucially, the mechanism only works if those who have the right to vote are not influenced or manipulated by any third parties. It is also necessary that every vote belongs to a different person or entity.

In the Sybil attack, an entity tries to manipulate a democratic choice by influencing other people's votes or by creating copies of its own vote so that it carries more weight. For example, an agent could manipulate an election site so that his votes were substituted with the real ones or so that voters were directly coerced into voting for his choice. In both cases, the democratic election does not truly represent the majority decision.

In the context of blockchain oracles, a Sybil attack refers to an agent's ability to control different oracles or create multiple identities to decide the data to be uploaded.

Sybil attacks can also be performed through *mirroring*. Mirroring is a technique whereby an entity that owns a multitude of oracles executes the data-fetching only once, and then simply mirrors the result to its other oracles, boosting the perceived trust of the chosen outcome as a result. When an average level of credibility is reached, this practice can be exploited to provide false data at favored times.

A recent study by John Douceur called "The Sybil Attack" underlines that, in a decentralized system, it is virtually impossible to prevent the Sybil attack. Irrespective of any security measures in place, if the voters' identities are not known, it is impossible to ensure that their votes are not manipulated.

To address the oracle problem, therefore, it is a necessary requirement that the oracle's identity be known and that their choices are always transparent.

A blockchain tutorial

This will be especially useful to those of you who prefer to get your hands dirty and learn by doing. One of my first blockchain teachers showed me a tutorial by Anders Brownworth that really caught my eye thanks to its clarity and comprehensiveness.

The tutorial can be found at the following link:

https://andersbrownworth.com/blockchain/

It has six sections, each of which explains interactively how blockchain works. I have included the sections on hash, blocks, and blockchain below.

Hash

The hash function serves to encrypt data into a string of characters that always have the same length. There are many different hash functions. The Bitcoin blockchain, for example, uses the hash function SHA256.

Here is an example of SHA256 in action.

SHA256 Hash

Here, we are asked to enter the data in the text box, and the hash will be generated below. (Even the empty box has its own hash.)

Here are some more examples with alternative data entries:

As you can see, no matter what is typed in the box, the length of the hash will always be the same. Also, just changing a single letter—from **B**itcoin to **b**itcoin to **ba**tcoin—will alter the generated hash completely. This is particularly helpful when ensuring that the data in a block has not been changed in any way. The same premise also applies to documents uploaded to the blockchain. As we saw with academic transcripts in Chapter 6, once a document is hashed, it is easy to spot any alterations (Of course, the system will only communicate that the document has been altered, but not how).

Blocks and blockchain

This section graphically shows the component parts of a block. Here is an example:

Block

There are four sections: Block, Nonce, Data, and Hash. The Block # corresponds to the block height, i.e., the distance from the genesis block. The Data section displays the transaction information (in this case, the transfer of Bitcoin). The Hash is the transaction data compressed using SHA256. Finally, the Nonce is the passphrase that miners have to find to validate the block. Since blocks are virtually infinite and nobody chooses the passphrase, the protocol specifies how it is possible to find the right one. Therefore, the nonce is the sequence of numbers that makes the hash start with a certain number of zeroes. The number of zeroes determines the difficulty level, which can be increased or decreased depending on the total computing power.

Block

Block:	# 1
Nonce:	6163
Data:	Alice sent 5 BTC to Albert Bob sent 2 BTC to Dylan Philip sent 0.5 BTC to Billy
Hash:	0000a81c98e0f42bf56a324f349b08f613efecb83ca4d861c5b322e6e73e786a

Mine

As you can see, by clicking on the "Mine" button, the nonce is calculated; as the hash starts with four zeroes, the passphrase is correct. The block turns green as it is considered "validated," and it is broadcast to the network so that other nodes can verify its validity.

In the first chapter, we discussed how the blockchain is immutable. In fact, if you have a full node, you might easily try to implement some modification to the block's content since it is directly in your possession.

Let's see what happens if someone modifies a block that has already been validated and broadcast to the network.

Block

Block:	# 1
Nonce:	6163
Data:	Alice sent 2 BTC to Albert Bob sent 2 BTC to Dylan Philip sent 0.5 BTC to Billy
Hash:	5211439e5512f3aa337ed9a1c017d55b7a47c6a08194a8e3ec2c3065a7f4e95f

Mine

Here is the block that was previously validated, but I've changed the amount of Bitcoin that Alice sent to Albert. As we know, even a slight adjustment to the data content completely changes the hash, so the block is now displayed as invalid (red background). The hash no longer starts with four zeroes, so the nonce (6163) is no longer the correct passphrase. Through this mechanism, the network can easily spot a tampered block and prevent its addition to the blockchain.

Now let's examine the case of a chain of blocks:

In this situation, all the blocks are already connected and validated. A crucial detail to note is that, along with transaction data, the previous block's hash concurs in forming the hash of the new block. This means that altering any single block will invalidate all subsequent blocks. Since all the resulting hashes change, the passphrases will no longer work:

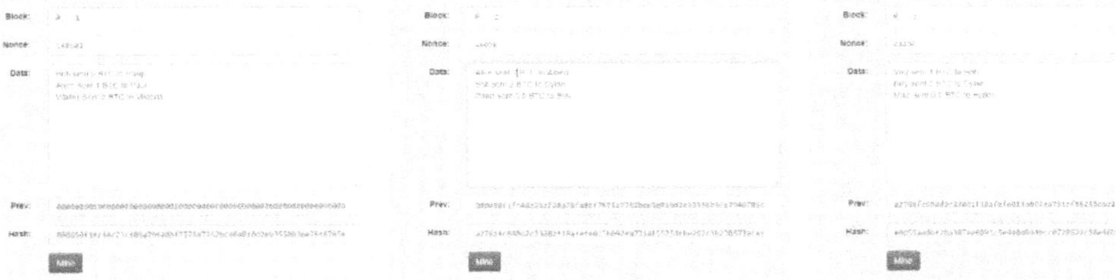

Just like the previous example, here I again changed the amount Alice sent to Albert. The block becomes invalid, and the following block (even though its content is unchanged) is invalidated as well. Since the previous hash data has changed, so too has the next in the chain.

Practice

The remaining tutorial sections are entitled "Distributed," "Tokens," and "Coinbase." You can easily check out those features yourself, and I strongly recommend doing so to better understand how the whole system works. Remember, though, that this is only intended as a simulator; the reality of blockchain is rather more technical and complex. The underlying premise, though, is captured brilliantly.

Happy simulation!

About the author

Personal mission

Not all that glitters is gold, but it is worth investigating!

My aim is to share knowledge on the real-world applications of blockchains from a business perspective. My personal area of focus is the subject of oracles and the oracle problem, because their relationship with trust particularly caught my attention.

Blockchain has the potential to disrupt the world as we know it, but if oracles are mishandled, blockchain will be disrupted instead. The limitations of blockchain when interacting with the real world are what divide promising projects from dangerous scams, so tackling the oracle problem should be our top priority.

Short biography

Born in the south of Italy, the author obtained his MBA at the University of Siena. Studying cybersecurity as a hobby, he worked as an IT consultant in northern Italy and the UK before entering academia. His current research focuses on blockchain oracles and real-world blockchains.

Academic research

For an updated list of my academic contributions, you can visit my personal page on Scopus, Google Scholar, or ResearchGate.

I look forward to your visit!

References, additional resources, and suggested readings

All the resources provided in this section were examined to write this book. However, I strongly recommend reading the original sources if you wish to study the subject further.

If time is short, the resources that are not to be avoided are the Bitcoin whitepaper, all the Andreas Antonopoulos books, and the Alexander Egberts paper on the oracle problem.

Happy reading!

Blockchain and Bitcoin

Antonopoulos, A.M. *Mastering Bitcoin: Programming the Open Blockchain*; 2nd ed.; O'Reilly, 2017

Antonopoulos, A.M. *The Internet of Money—Volume Three*; Merkle Bloom LLC: Seattle, WA, USA, 2019.

Antonopoulos, A.M. *The Internet of Money—Volume Two*; Merkle Bloom LLC: Seattle, WA, USA, 2018.

Antonopoulos, A.M. *The Internet of Money*; Merkle Bloom LLC: Seattle, WA, USA, 2016.

Buterin, V. On Public and Private Blockchains. *Ethereum Blog*. 6 August 2015. Available online: https://blog.ethereum.org/2015/08/07/on-public-and-private-blockchains/ (accessed on 11 December 2019).

Cohney, S.; Hoffman, D.A.; Sklaroff, J.; Wishnick, D. Coin-Operated Capitalism. *Columbia Law Rev.* **2019**, *119*, 591.

DiStefano, J. N. (2017, February 2). Blockchain: 'A novel solution to the problem of trust' beyond Bitcoin. Retrieved from The Inquirer Daily News: http://www.philly.com/philly/blogs/inq-phillydeals/Blockchain-.html

Haber, S.; Stornetta, S. How to timestamp a digital document—Original blockchain paper 1991. *J. Cryptol.* **1991**, *3*, 99–111.

He, D.; Habermeier, K.; Leckow, R.; Haksar, V.; Almeida, Y.; Kashima, M.; Kyriakos-Saad, N.; Oura, H.; Sedik, T.S.; Stetsenko, N.; et al. *Virtual Currencies and Beyond: Initial Considerations*; No. 16/3; International Monetary Fund: Washington, DC, USA, 2016.

Jamison, M.A.; Tariq, P. Five things regulators should know about blockchain (and three myths to forget). *Electr. J.* **2018**, *31*, 20–23.

Locher, T.; Obermeier, S.; Pignolet, Y.A. When Can a Distributed Ledger Replace a Trusted Third Party? In Proceedings of the Proceedings - IEEE 2018

International Congress on Cybermatics: 2018 IEEE Conferences on Internet of Things, Green Computing and Communications, Cyber, Physical and Social Computing, Smart Data, Blockchain, Computer and Information Technology, iThings/Gree; 2018; pp. 1069–1077.

Madan, C.; Sinha, A.; Sharma, K. Success of blockchain and bitcoin. *Int. J. Recent Technol. Eng.* **2019**, *7*.

Nakamoto, S. Bitcoin: A Peer-to-Peer Electronic Cash System. 2008. 9p. Available online: https://bitcoin.org/bitcoin.pdf (accessed on 29 October 2020).

Nofer, M.; Gomber, P.; Hinz, O.; Schiereck, D. Blockchain. Bus. Inf. Syst. Eng. 2017, 59, 183–187, doi:10.1007/s12599-017-0467-3.

Perego, A.; Sciuto, D.; Portale, V.; Bruschi, F. Blockchain & Distributed Ledger 2019. Available online: https://www.osservatori.net/it_it/osservatori/blockchain-distributed-ledger (accessed on 13 December 2019).

Sharma, T.K. PUBLIC VS. PRIVATE BLOCKCHAIN : A COMPREHENSIVE COMPARISON Available online: https://www.blockchain-council.org/blockchain/public-vs-private-blockchain-a-comprehensive-comparison/ (accessed on Dec 13, 2020).

Sui, D.; Ricci, S.; Pfeffer, J. Are Miners Centralized? A Look into Mining Pools. Available online: https://media.consensys.net/are-miners-centralized-a-look-into-mining-pools-b594425411dc (accessed on 29 October 2020).

Swan, M. *Blockchain Blueprint for a New Economy*; O'Reilly Media: Sebastopol, CA, USA, 2005.

Tasca, P.; Tessone, C.J. A Taxonomy of Blockchain Technologies: Principles of Identification and Classification. *Ledger* **2019**, *4*, 1–39.

Yli-Huumo, J.; Ko, D.; Choi, S.; Park, S.; Smolander, K. Where is Current Research on Blockchain Technology?—A Systematic Review. *PLoS ONE* **2016**, *11*, e0163477.

Zavolokina, L.; Schwabe, G.; Bauer, I. To Token or Not to Token: Tools for Understanding Blockchain Tokens. In Proceedings of the Thirty Ninth International Conference on Information Systems, San Francisco, CA, USA, 13–16 December 2018.

Smart Contracts and Ethereum

Antonopoulos, A.M.; Woods, G. *Mastering Ethereum—Building Smart Contracts and DAPPS*; O'Reilly: Sebastopol, CA, USA, 2018.

Bartoletti, M., & Pompianu, L. (2017, March 18). An empirical analysis of smart contracts: platforms, applications, and design patterns. Retrieved from Cornell University Library: https://arxiv.org/abs/1703.06322

Buterin, V. (2014, July 22). Ethereum and Oracles. Retrieved from Ethereum Blog: https://blog.ethereum.org/2014/07/22/ethereum-and-oracles/

Buterin, V. (2014, March 28). SchellingCoin: A Minimal-Trust Universal Data Feed. Retrieved from Ethereum Blog: https://blog.ethereum.org/2014/03/28/schellingcoin-a-minimal-trust-universal-data-feed/

Buterin, V. Ethereum: A Next-Generation Smart Contract and Decentralized Application Platform. Available online: https://github.com/ethereum/wiki/wiki/White-Paper (accessed on 12 April 2020).

Cuccuru, P. Beyond bitcoin: An early overview on smart contracts. *Int. J. Law Inf. Technol.* **2017**, *25*, 179–195, doi:10.1093/ijlit/eax003.

Evans, J. (2016, May 22). All the cool kids are doing Ethereum now. Retrieved from techchrunch.com: https://techcrunch.com/2016/05/22/all-the-cool-kids-are-doing-ethereum-now/

F. (2014, December 12). What are Smart Contracts? In search of a consensus. Retrieved from Medium: https://medium.com/@heckerhut/whats-a-smart-contract-in-search-of-a-consensus-c268c830a8ad

Graham, R. Ethereum/TheDAO Hack Simplified. Available online: https://blog.erratasec.com/2016/06/etheriumdao-hack-similfied.html (accessed on 14 April 2020).

Hertig, A. (2017, July 8.). Smart Contracts for Bitcoin? Lightning's Tadge Dryja Is Working on It. Retrieved from Coindesk: https://www.coindesk.com/smart-contracts-bitcoin-lightnings-tadge-dryja-working/

Kovačević, A. Ethereum 2.0 Includes Major Changes That Could End Bitcoin's Blockchain Dominance Available online: https://www.computer.org/publications/tech-news/trends/end-bitcoins-blockchain-dominance (accessed on Sep 2, 2020).

Millman, R. What is Ethereum 2.0 and Why Does It Matter? Available online: https://decrypt.co/resources/what-is-ethereum-2-0 (accessed on Dec 11, 2020).

Molecke, R. (2017, June). How To Learn Solidity: The Ultimate Ethereum Coding Guide. Retrieved from blockgeeks.com: https://blockgeeks.com/guides/how-to-learn-solidity/

Silva, D.M. Ethereum Classic is Under Attack. Available online: https://qz.com/1516994/ethereum-classic-got-hit-by-a-51-attack/ (accessed on 12 March 2020).

Subramanian, H. Security tokens: architecture, smart contract applications and illustrations using SAFE. Manag. Financ. 2019, doi:10.1108/MF-09-2018-0467.

Thomson, C. The DAO of ETHEREUM: Analyzing the DAO Hack, the Blockchain, Smart Contracts, and the Law. Available online: https://medium.com/blockchain-review/the-dao-of-ethereum-e228b93afc79 (accessed on 3 April 2020).

Oracles and Oracle Problem

Antonopoulos, A.M. The Killer App: Bananas on the Blockchain? Available online: https://aantonop.com/the-killer-app-bananas-on-theblockchain (accessed on 3 March 2020).

Apla What Is a Blockchain Oracle? Available online: https://blog.apla.io/what-is-a-blockchain-oracle-2ccca433c026 (accessed on 1 March 2020).

Barr, E.T.; Harman, M.; McMinn, P.; Shahbaz, M.; Yoo, S. The Oracle Problem in Software Testing: A Survey. *IEEE Trans. Softw. Eng.* **2015**, *41*, 507–525.

Buck, J. Blockchain Oracles Explained. Available online: https://cointelegraph.com/explained/blockchain-oracles-explained (accessed on 1 March 2020).

Caldarelli, G. Real-world blockchain applications under the lens of the oracle problem. A systematic literature review. In Proceedings of the IEEE International Conference on Technology Management, Operations and Decisions, Marrakech, Morocco, 25–27 November 2020.

Caldarelli, G. Understanding the Blockchain Oracle Problem : A Call for Action. *Information* **2020**, *11*, doi:10.3390/info11110509.

Caldarelli, G.; Rossignoli, C.; Zardini, A. Overcoming the blockchain oracle problem in the traceability of non-fungible products. *Sustainability* **2020**, *12*, 2391.

Curran, B. What Are Oracles? Smart Contracts, Chainlink & "The Oracle Problem. Available online: https://blockonomi.com/oracles-guide (accessed on 29 October 2020).

Dalovindj, U. The Oracle Problem. Available online: https://www.reddit.com/r/Bitcoin/comments/2p78kd/the_oracle_problem/ (accessed on 2 March 2020).

Damjan, M. The interface between blockchain and the real world. *Ragion Prat.* **2018**, *2018*, 379–406.

Davis, J. A Discussion of the Oracle Problem. 2019. Available online: https://hackernoon.com/a-discussion-of-the-oracle-problem-6cbec7872c10 (accessed on 11 December 2019).

Egberts, A. The Oracle Problem—An Analysis of how Blockchain Oracles Undermine the Advantages of Decentralized Ledger Systems. *SSRN Electron. J.* **2017**.

Frankenreiter, J. The limits of smart contracts. *J. Inst. Theor. Econ.* **2019**, *175*, 149–162.

Galson, S. The Oracle Problem. Available online: https://www.yld.io/blog/the-oracle-problem/ (accessed on 2 March 2020).

Guadamuz, A. All watched over by machines of loving grace: A critical look at smart contracts. *Comput. Law Secur. Rev.* **2019**, *35*, 105338.

Kim, H.M.; Laskowski, M. Toward an ontology-driven blockchain design for supply-chain provenance. *Intell. Syst. Account. Financ. Manag.* **2018**, *25*, 18–27.

Liu, H.; Kuo, F.-C.; Towey, D.; Chen, T.Y. How Effectively Does Metamorphic Testing Alleviate the Oracle Problem? *IEEE Trans. Softw. Eng.* **2014**, *40*, 4–22.

Pastore, F.; Mariani, L.; Fraser, G. CrowdOracles: Can the Crowd Solve the Oracle Problem? In Proceedings of the 2013 IEEE Sixth International Conference on Software Testing, Verification and Validation, Luxembourg, 18–22 March 2013; IEEE: Luxembourg, 2013; pp. 342–351.

Patrick, C. What Is a Blockchain Oracle? Available online: https://medium.com/better-programming/what-is-a-blockchain-oracle-f5ccab8dbd72 (accessed on 21 October 2020).

R. Van Mölken, Blockchain Across Oracle: Understand Details Implications Blockchain for Oracle Developers Customers. Birmingham, U.K.: Packt Publishing, 2018.

Ramachandran, A.; Kantarcioglu, D.M. Using Blockchain and smart contracts for secure data provenance management. *arXiv* **2017**, arXiv:1709.10000.

Schaad, A.; Reski, T.; Winzenried, O. Integration of a Secure Physical Element as a Trusted Oracle in a Hyperledger Blockchain. In Proceedings of the 16th Internationla Joint Conference on e-Business and Telecommunications, Prague, Czech Republic, 26–28 July 2019; SCITEPRESS—Science and Technology Publications: Prague, Czech Republic, 2019; pp. 498–503.

Song, J. The Truth about Smart Contracts. Available online: https://medium.com/@jimmysong/the-truth-about-smart-contracts-ae825271811f (accessed on 2 March 2020).

Szabo, N. Formalizing and Securing Relationships on Public Networks. Available online: https://journals.uic.edu/ojs/index.php/fm/article/view/548 (accessed on 15 February 2020).

Sztorc, P. The Oracle Problem. Available online: https://www.infoq.com/presentations/blockchain-oracle-problems (accessed on 3 March 2020).

Tsankov, A. The "Oracle Problem" isn't a Problem, and Why Smart Contracts Makes Insurance Better for Everyone. Available online: https://medium.com/@antsankov/the-oracle-problem-isnt-a-problem-and-why-smart-contracts-makes-insurance-better-for-everyone-8c979f09851c (accessed on 2 March 2020).

Oracle Providers

A. S. de Pedro, D. Levi, and L. I. Cuende, "Witnet: A decentralized oracle network protocol," 2017, arXiv:1711.09756. [Online]. Available: http://arxiv.org/abs/1711.09756

Al-Breiki, H.; Rehman, M.H.U.; Salah, K.; Svetinovic, D. Trustworthy Blockchain Oracles: Review, Comparison, and Open Research Challenges. IEEE Access 2020, 8, 85675–85685, doi:10.1109/ACCESS.2020.2992698.

Dale, O. What Is Chainlink? Guide to The Decentralized Oracle Network. Available online: https://blockonomi.com/chainlink-guide/ (accessed on 12 March 2020).

Ellis, S., Jules, A., & Nazarov, S. (2017, September 4). ChainLink - A Decentralized Oracle Network. Retrieved from smartcontract.com: https://link.smartcontract.com/whitepaper

Ether Wager. (2017, August 5). Introducing Oracul: Decentralized Oracle Data Feed Solution for Ethereum. Retrieved from Medium:

https://medium.com/@roman.brodetski/introducing-oracul-decentralized-oracle-data-feed-solution-for-ethereum-5cab1ca8bb64

Harper, C. What Is ChainLink? A Beginner's Guide to Decentralized Oracles. Available online: https://coincentral.com/what-is-chainlink-a-beginners-guide-to-decentralized-oracles/ (accessed on 12 March 2020).

J. Adler, R. Berryhill, A. Veneris, Z. Poulos, N. Veira, and A. Kastania, "'Astraea: A decentralized blockchain oracle," in Proc. IEEE Int. Conf. Internet Things (iThings) IEEE Green Comput. Commun. (GreenCom) IEEE Cyber, Phys. Social Comput. (CPSCom) IEEE Smart Data (SmartData), Jul. 2018, pp. 1145–1152.

J. Peterson, J. Krug, M. Zoltu, A. K. Williams, and S. Alexander, "Augur: A decentralized oracle and prediction market platform," 2015, arXiv:1501.01042. [Online]. Available: http://arxiv.org/abs/1501.01042

Petersen, D. J., & Krug, J. (2014). Augur: a Decentralized, Open-Source Platform for Prediction Markets. Retrieved from Bravenewcoin.com: https://bravenewcoin.com/assets/Whitepapers/Augur-A-Decentralized-Open-Source-Platform-for-Prediction-Markets.pdf

R. Berryhill and A. Veneris, "ASTRAEA: A decentralized blockchain oracle," IEEE Blockchain Tech. Briefs, vol. 2, no. 2, Mar. 2019.

S. Ellis, A. Juels, and S. Nazarov, "ChainLink: A decentralized oracle network," White Paper, Mar. 2017, vol. 11, p. 2018. [Online]. Available: https://link.smartcontract.com/whitepaper

Shawdagor, J. Solve.Care Partners with Chainlink to Revolutionize the Healthcare Sector. Available online: https://invezz.com/news/2020/10/20/solve-care-partners-with-chainlink-to-revolutionize-the-healthcare-sector/ (accessed on 22 October 2020).

Z. Hess, Y. Malahov, and J. Pettersson. (2017). Aeternity Blockchain. [Online]. Available: https://aeternity.com/aeternityblockchainwhitepaper.pdf

Zhang, F., Cecchetti, E., Croman, K., Juels, A., & Shi, E. (2016, October 15). Town Crier: An Authenticated Data Feed for Smart Contracts. Retrieved from Cornell University: The Initiative for CryptoCurrencies & Contracts: http://www.initc3.org/publications.html

Zhang, F.; Cecchetti, E.; Croman, K.; Juels, A.; Shi, E. Town Crier: An Authenticated Data Feed for Smart Contracts. Available online: https://eprint.iacr.org/2016/168.pdf (accessed on 5 March 2020).

Real-World Blockchains

Alharby, M.; van Moorsel, A. Blockchain Based Smart Contracts: A Systematic Mapping Study. *arXiv* **2017**, arXiv:1710.06372.

Arizona House Bill 2417: Signatures; Electronic Transactions; Blockchain Technology; House of Representatives: Washington, DC, USA, 2017; pp. 1–3.

Azaria, A.; Ekblaw, A.; Vieira, T.; Lippman, A. MedRec: Using blockchain for medical data access and permission management. In Proceedings of the 2016 2nd International Conference on Open and Big Data (OBD), Vienna, Austria, 22–24 August 2016; pp. 25–30.

Bdiwi, R.; De Runz, C.; Faiz, S.; Cherif, A.A. Towards a New Ubiquitous Learning Environment Based on Blockchain Technology. In Proceedings of the Proceedings—IEEE 17th International Conference on Advanced Learning Technologies, ICALT 2017, Timisoara, Romania, 3–7 July 2017; pp. 101–102.

Ben Fekih, R.; Lahami, M. *Application of Blockchain Technology in Healthcare: A Comprehensive Study*; Springer International Publishing: New York, NY, USA, 2020; Volume 12157, ISBN 9783030515164.

Brownsword, R. Regulatory Fitness: Fintech, Funny Money, and Smart Contracts. *Eur. Bus. Organ. Law Rev.* **2019**, *20*, 5–27.

Caldarelli, G. Exploiting Corporate Governance to Evaluate Blockchain Applications : A Comprehensive Framework. Int. J. Econ. Bus. Adm. 2020, VIII, 166–183.

Caldarelli, G.; Ellul, J. Trusted Academic Transcripts on the Blockchain: A Systematic Literature Review. *Appl. Sci.* **2021**, *11*, 1842. https://doi.org/10.3390/app11041842

Camilleri, A.G.A.F. *Blockchain in Education*; Publications Office of the European Union: Luxembourg, 2017; ISBN 9789279734977.

Desk, A.N. Solve.Care Collaborates With Chainlink To Deliver Real-World Data For Blockchain Healthcare Services. Available online: https://aithority.com/technology/blockchain/solve-care-collaborates-with-chainlink-to-deliver-real-world-data-for-blockchain-healthcare-services/ (accessed on 20 October 2020).

Donald, T. The Most Promising Blockchain Healthcare Projects. 2020. Available online: https://blog.lumiwallet.com/the-most-promising-blockchain-healthcare-projects-2020/ (accessed on 20 October 2020).

Gerard, D. The World Food Programme's Much Publicized "Blockchain" Has One Participant—i.e., It's a Database. Available online: https://davidgerard.co.uk/blockchain/2017/11/26/the-world-food-programmes-much-publicised-blockchain-has-one-participant-i-e-its-a-database/ (accessed on 17 March 2020).

Hasselgren, A.; Kralevska, K.; Gligoroski, D.; Pedersen, S.A.; Faxvaag, A. Blockchain in healthcare and health sciences—A scoping review. *Int. J. Med. Inform.* **2020**, *134*, 104040.

Hou, J.; Wang, H.; Liu, P. Applying the blockchain technology to promote the development of distributed photovoltaic in China. *Int. J. Energy Res.* **2018**, *42*, 2050–2069.

Jeffries, A. "Blockchain" Is Meaningless. Available online: https://www.theverge.com/2018/3/7/17091766/blockchain-bitcoin-ethereum-cryptocurrency-meaning (accessed on 19 April 2020).

Jirgensons, M.; Kapenieks, J. Blockchain and the Future of Digital Learning Credential

Assessment and Management. *J. Teach. Educ. Sustain.* **2018**, *20*, 145–156.

Li, Z.; Bahramirad, S.; Paaso, A.; Yan, M.; Shahidehpour, M. Blockchain for decentralized transactive energy management system in networked microgrids. *Electr. J.* **2019**, *32*, 58–72.

Lielacher, A. Top Blockchain Healthcare Projects for 2020, Rated and Reviewed. Available online: https://www.bitcoinmarketjournal.com/top-blockchain-healthcare-projects-for-2019-rated-and-reviewed/ (accessed on 21 October 2020).

Low, K.F.K.; Mik, E. Pause the blockchain legal revolution. *Int. Comp. Law Q.* **2019**, *69*, 135–175.

McCoy, T.H.; Perlis, R.H. Temporal trends and characteristics of reportable health data breaches, 2010–2017. *JAMA-J. Am. Med. Assoc.* **2018**, *320*, 1282–1284.

Meinert, E.; Alturkistani, A.; Foley, K.A.; Osama, T.; Car, J.; Majeed, A.; Van Velthoven, M.; Wells, G.; Brindley, D. Blockchain implementation in health care: Protocol for a systematic review. *J. Med. Internet Res.* **2019**, *21*, e12439.

Mengelkamp, E.; Gärttner, J.; Weinhardt, C. Decentralizing energy systems through local energy markets: The LAMP-project. In Proceedings of the MKWI 2018—Multikonferenz Wirtschaftsinformatik, Lüneburg, Deutschland, 6–9 March 2018; Volume 2018, pp. 924–930.

Mik, E. Smart contracts: Terminology, technical limitations and real world complexity. *Law Innov. Technol.* **2017**, *9*, 269–300.

Morkunas, V.J.; Paschen, J.; Boon, E. How blockchain technologies impact your business model. *Bus. Horiz.* **2019**, *62*, 295–306.

Mougayar, W. *The Business Blockchain: Promise, Practice, and Application of the Next Internet Technology*; John Wiley & Sons Inc.: Hoboken, NJ, USA, 2016.

Radanović, I.; Likić, R. Opportunities for Use of Blockchain Technology in Medicine. *Appl. Health Econ. Health Policy* **2018**, *16*, 583–590.

Rensaa, J.A.H.; Gligoroski, D.; Kralevska, K.; Hasselgren, A.; Faxvaag, A. VerifyMed-A blockchain platform for transparent trust in virtualized healthcare: Proof-of-concept. In Proceedings of the 2020 2nd International Electronics Communication Conference, IECC 2020, Singapore, 8–10 July 2020; pp. 73–80.

Rupasinghe, T.; Burstein, F.; Rudolph, C.; Strange, S. Towards a Blockchain based Fall Prediction Model for Aged Care. In Proceedings of the Australasian Computer Science Week Multiconference, Sydney, NSW, Australia, 29–31 January 2019.

Sawa, T. Blockchain technology outline and its application to field of power and energy system. *Electr. Eng. Jpn.* **2019**, *206*, 11–15.

Shatkovskaya, T.V.; Shumilina, A.B.; Nebratenko, G.G.; Isakova, J.I.; Sapozhnikova, E.Y. Impact of technological blockchain paradigm on the movement of intellectual property in the digital space. *Eur. Res. Stud. J.* **2018**, *21*, 397–406.

Swan, M. *Blockchain: Bluepring for a New Economy*, 1st ed.; O'Reilly: Sebastopol, CA, USA, 2015.

Talesh, S.A. Data Breach, Privacy, and Cyber Insurance: How Insurance Companies Act as "Compliance Managers" for Businesses. *Law Soc. Inq.* **2018**, *43*, 417–440.

Tandon, A.; Dhir, A.; Islam, N.; Mäntymäki, M. Blockchain in healthcare: A systematic literature review, synthesizing framework and future research agenda. *Comput. Ind.* **2020**, *122*, 103290.

Treiblmaier, H. The impact of the blockchain on the supply chain: A theory-based research framework and a call for action. *Supply Chain Manag. Int. J.* **2018**, *23*, 545–559.

Wu, J.; Tran, N.K. Application of blockchain technology in sustainable energy systems: An overview. *Sustainability* **2018**, *10*, 3067.

Yong, B.; Shen, J.; Liu, X.; Li, F.; Chen, H.; Zhou, Q. An intelligent blockchain-based system for safe vaccine supply and supervision. *Int. J. Inf. Manag.* **2020**, *52*, 102024.